THE INTERNATIONAL JOURNAL FOR THE PSYCHOLOGY OF RELIGION, *10*(1), 1

EDITOR'S NOTE

One of the most important concepts in the history of psychology is intelligence. Over 100 years ago, early attempts to define intelligence were established and became the precursor for the entire field of mental testing and set the direction for much of the field of psychology. Traditionally, intelligence has been thought of as a more or less unitary mental capacity, connoting a general problem-solving ability and skill at abstract reasoning. More recently, a major counter-argument to the idea that intelligence is unitary was published by Howard Gardner (1993) in *Frames of Mind: The Theory of Multiple Intelligences*. In his view, intelligence is not a unitary construct but instead is multidimensional, comprised of linguistic, musical, logical–mathematical, spatial, bodily–kinesthetic, interpersonal, and intrapersonal facets. Since then, a dialog has continued about what does and does not constitute an intelligence.

In the lead article to this issue, Robert Emmons argues that the concept of spirituality, correctly understood as a psychological construct, constitutes an intelligence and meets Gardner's criteria for such. His article is followed by three commentaries, each by a scholar renowned in the area. Howard Gardner discusses the issues involved in the article by Emmons, highlighting a case against spiritual intelligence. Susan Kwilecki applies the arguments and issues to the analysis of a single case, and asks the question, "How do we know whether this individual does or does not have a high degree of spiritual intelligence?" John Mayer draws an insightful distinction between spiritual intelligence and spiritual consciousness, and explores the question of which concept is or ought to be the dominant one. The three commentaries are each given an in-depth, thoughtful response by Robert Emmons in the closing article. It is clear that his goal of provoking discussion and debate about the legitimacy of the concept of spiritual intelligence and its implications for the psychology of religion was achieved.

It is my pleasure to publish this special issue of the journal with the hope that it stimulates scholarship and research on these important issues.

Raymond F. Paloutzian
Editor, *IJPR*
Westmont College

THE INTERNATIONAL JOURNAL FOR THE PSYCHOLOGY OF RELIGION, *10*(1), 3–26

INVITED ESSAY

Is Spirituality an Intelligence? Motivation, Cognition, and the Psychology of Ultimate Concern

Robert A. Emmons

Department of Psychology
University of California, Davis

This article explores spirituality as a form of intelligence. The evidence for spirituality as a set of capacities and abilities that enable people to solve problems and attain goals in their everyday lives is evaluated. Five components of spiritual intelligence are identified: (a) the capacity for transcendence; (b) the ability to enter into heightened spiritual states of consciousness; (c) the ability to invest everyday activities, events, and relationships with a sense of the sacred; (d) the ability to utilize spiritual resources to solve problems in living; and (e) the capacity to engage in virtuous behavior (to show forgiveness, to express gratitude, to be humble, to display compassion). Evidence that spirituality meets the criteria for an intelligence is reviewed. Implications of studying spirituality within an intelligence framework are discussed.

In this article, I advance the argument that spirituality might be conceived of as a type of intelligence. Evidence for spirituality as a set of interrelated abilities and skills is considered. I contend that a serious consideration of the overlap between intelligence and spirituality may yield previously neglected theoretical and practical dividends. A spiritual intelligence framework has the potential to both integrate disparate research findings in the psychology of religion and spirituality and generate new research yielding fresh insights into the spiritual basis of behavior.

Requests for reprints should be sent to Robert A. Emmons, Department of Psychology, University of California, One Shields Avenue, Davis, CA 95616–8686. E-mail: raemmons@ucdavis.edu

The many meanings of spirituality and religiousness have recently become the focus of vigorous theoretical and empirical scrutiny. At the same time, emerging trends in the psychology of religion have yielded an impressive but as of yet unintegrated account of adaptive functioning, in which spiritual beliefs, commitments, and practices have been associated with a wide variety of criteria of success in living including physical health, psychological well-being, and marital satisfaction and stability. A concept that has the potential to unite these various literatures would be serving an important integrative function. Spiritual intelligence might be one such integrative concept.

SPIRITUALITY AS ULTIMATE CONCERN

Spirituality is the personal expression of ultimate concern. Tillich (1957) contended that the essence of religion, in the broadest and most inclusive sense, is the state of being ultimately concerned—having a "passion for the infinite," a passion that is unparalleled in human motivation. Religion "is the state of being grasped by an ultimate concern, a concern which qualifies all other concerns as preliminary and which itself contains the answer to the question of the meaning of our life" (Tillich, 1963, p. 4). Similarly, Heschel (1955) depicted the search for God as "the search for ultimacy" (p. 125), and Allport (1950) defined a mature religious sentiment as "a disposition to respond favorably ... to objects or principles that the individual regards as of *ultimate importance* in his own life, and as having to do with what he regards as permanent or central in the nature of things" (p. 56). Spirituality has been defined as that which "involves ultimate and personal truths" (Wong, 1998, p. 364), and spirituality refers to how an individual "lives meaningfully with ultimacy, his or her response to the deepest truths of the universe" (Bregman & Thierman, 1995, p. 149).

In a recent book (Emmons, 1999), I described a research program devoted to studying the presence of ultimate concerns through personal goal strivings. Personal strivings represent what people are typically trying to do, their "signature" goal pursuits. There is an intimate connection between religion and goals. One of the functions of a religious belief system and a religious world view is that it provides "an ultimate vision of what people should be striving for in their lives" (Pargament & Park, 1995, p. 15), as providing a guide to "the most serious and far-ranging goals there can possibly be" (Apter, 1985, p. 69). There is a long history of using goal language metaphorically to depict spiritual growth. In devotional writings, spiritual growth and spiritual maturity are viewed as processes of goal attainment, with the ultimate goal being intimacy with the divine. It is, therefore, ultimate concern that shapes and gives direction to a person's ultimate concerns in life. Spiritual strivings, then, as personal goals focused on the sacred, become the way in which ultimate concerns are encountered in people's lives. Ultimate concerns are bridges linking motivation, spirituality, and intelligence.

The personal striving approach has its roots in cognitive personality theory. The basic assumptions of the cognitive–motivational approach to personality are the following. People are intentional, (usually) rational beings who are engaged in a constant effort to strive toward personal meaningfully defined goals. These goals emerge as a function of internal propensities such as motive dispositions and basic needs in concert with cultural demands and situational affordances that shape their expression across situations and over time. Motivation in the form of goal-directedness is a major component of the cognitive approach, and motivation is a key aspect of personality as it lends coherence and patterning to people's behavior. Motivational units, such as goals, motives, and values, form a hierarchical system of which various levels could be activated depending on environmental stimuli.

INTELLIGENCE, PERSONALITY, AND ADAPTIVE FUNCTIONING

The cognitive–motivational perspective on which the personal striving framework is situated opened the door for a reconceptualization of the role of intelligence in personality. A recent volume (Sternberg & Ruzgis, 1994) dedicated to the interface of intelligence and personality contained contributions from a number of distinguished researchers in these respective fields. They explored a number of important interdependencies between intelligence and personality processes, many of which also pertain to the study of intelligence and spiritual processes.

Ford (1994) highlighted four basic questions that should be asked about human functioning. He referred to these as the process question, the content question, the effectiveness question, and the developmental question. These four questions are at the heart of personality psychology, and two are directly the focus of this article. The content question addresses the "what" or the having side of personality—what is the substance or meaning of a person's thoughts, goals, and actions? Spirituality and religion are important domains of goal striving for most people (Emmons, 1999). The effectiveness question deals with how well the person is functioning according to some criteria of success in life—happiness, life satisfaction, personality integration, and the like. Ford contended that intelligence is the most commonly employed construct used to address the effectiveness question. Intelligence, then, is defined as "the characteristic of a person's functioning associated with the attainment of relevant goals within some specified set of contexts and evaluative boundary conditions" (p. 203).

Defining Intelligence

There is little agreement over how to define *intelligence* (Neisser et al., 1996; Sternberg, 1997). Many conceptions equate intelligence with adaptive problem-solving behavior, where problem solving is defined with respect to practical goal attainment and some sort of positive developmental outcome. According to Sternberg (1990), the adaptiveness of intelligent behavior is viewed in light of whether it can function to meet the goals of the organism. Intelligence was recently defined as "the level of skills and knowledge currently available for problem-solving" (Chiu, Hong, & Dweck, 1994, p. 106), "the ability to attain goals in the face of obstacles by means of decisions based on rational rules" (Pinker, 1997, p. 62), as "a set of abilities that permits an individual to solve problems or fashion products that are of consequence in a particular cultural setting" (Walters & Gardner, 1986, p. 164), and "mental abilities necessary for adaptation to ... any environmental context" (Sternberg, 1997, p. 1036). Problem solving is inherently goal-directed—identifying a goal, locating and pursuing appropriate routes to the goal, and organizing potentially competing goals so as to maximize joint attainment are problem-solving skills needed for the effective negotiation of one's adaptive landscape. Goal setting creates a series of problems to be solved, as it requires the formulation of strategies and plans to pursue these goals in the face of external obstacles or internal obstacles such as frustration, depression, anxiety, and conflict with other pursuits. For example, the ultimate concern of living a life that is pleasing to God requires an identification of and commitment to a lifestyle that is pleasing to God, an identification of and a commitment to avoid that which is displeasing to God, and inner self-regulatory mechanisms to deal with frustrations, temptations, and setbacks that will inevitably occur in trying to live a responsible and accountable life of this type in an environment that may lack supports for such efforts.

The central theme behind these definitions of intelligence is a focus on adaptive problem solving. The issues of what constitutes adaptive functioning and what is required to function adaptively are important ones. Dweck (1990) specified a set of three criteria to distinguish adaptive from maladaptive functioning. First, an adaptive pattern should minimize the potential for goal conflict. Competing goals compromise effective functioning and are a major source of psychological and physical stress (Emmons & King, 1988). The goal of living a life that is pleasing to God could easily come into conflict with self-serving goals. Adaptiveness implies, among other attributes, the coordination of multiple goals in the service of higher order principles. The second criterion of an adaptive pattern is that it should enhance the probability of goal attainment. Third, an adaptive pattern should allow a person to effectively utilize a maximum amount of available information.

Ford (1994) listed four prerequisites for effective functioning: *motivation*, which determines the content of goal-directed action; *skills*, which produce the desired consequences of movement toward goals; *biological architecture*, which supports the motivational and skill components; and a *supportive environment* (or at least one that is nonhindering), which facilitates progress toward the goal. Intelligent behavior, then, requires "a motivated, skillful person whose biological and behavioral capabilities support relevant interactions with an environment that has the informational and material properties and resources needed to facilitate (or at least permit) goal attainment" (p. 203). Intelligence within specific domains is revealed by the following: breadth of knowledge, depth of knowledge, performance accomplishments, automaticity or ease of functioning, skilled performance under challenging conditions, generative flexibility, and speed of learning and developmental change.

THE THEORY OF MULTIPLE INTELLIGENCES

One of the most influential and widespread theories of intelligence is Gardner's theory of multiple intelligences (MI; Gardner, 1993, 1995, 1996; Walters & Gardner, 1986). Gardner's theory is not the only approach to intelligence currently in vogue (see Neisser et al., 1996, for an overview of some contemporary perspectives). However, I have chosen it here for three primary reasons: (a) because of its popularity and familiarity among psychologists, educators, and laity; (b) because of the comprehensive set of criteria Gardner specified to evaluate a candidate intelligence; and (c) because in published articles on MI theory Gardner debated the merits of spirituality as an intelligence.

As described earlier, Gardner (1993, 1995, 1996; Walters & Gardner, 1986) defined intelligence as a set of abilities that are used to solve problems and fashion products that are valuable within a particular cultural setting or community. He postulated a number of relatively autonomous intellectual capacities, eight in all. They exist as potentials inherent in each person, yet vary genetically in terms of individual competencies and potential for development. The eight distinct intelligences are linguistic, logical–mathematical, spatial, musical, bodily–kinesthetic, interpersonal, intrapersonal, and naturalist. Each intelligence is a system in itself, distinct from a global, unified entity of generalized intelligence. He argued that these separate intelligences exist on the basis of their cultural significance and their correspondence to underlying neural structures. Gardner (1993) presented evidence for the existence of these separate computational or information processing systems and suggests that cultures differentially structure conditions to maximize the development of specific competencies in their members.

In order to determine what competencies and abilities qualify as an intelligence, Gardner (1993) laid out eight criteria for distinguishing an independent intelligence:

1. An identifiable core operation or set of operations.
2. An evolutionary history and evolutionary plausibility.
3. A characteristic pattern of development.
4. Potential isolation by brain damage.
5. The existence of persons distinguished by the exceptional presence or absence of the ability.
6. Susceptibility to encoding in a symbol system.

7. Support from experimental psychological investigations.
8. Support from psychometric findings.

Although the list of intelligences is negotiable, these eight criteria are not. For a human capacity to be considered an intelligence in the MI framework, it must satisfy the majority of the criteria.

Should spirituality be considered part of the human intellectual repertoire? Is there a spiritual information processing system comparable to the other intelligences? What would happen if Gardner's (1993) criteria for the existence of an intelligence were applied to spirituality? I argue that a legitimate case can be made for spirituality as a set of related competencies and abilities that provide a reasonable fit to the eight criteria. My impression is that a narrow definition of spirituality led Gardner to a premature dismissal of the possibility of considering spirituality as a form of intelligence. Given the interest that the constructs of intelligence and spirituality attract, a fair-minded examination of the empirical data is warranted. Before we examine spiritual intelligence vis-à-vis Gardner's criteria, the nature of what constitutes spiritual intelligence needs to be fleshed out.

Spirituality in the Theory of Multiple Intelligences

In his writings on MI theory, Gardner (1996) made it clear that spirituality is not one of the intelligences. For instance, "I cannot enumerate how often I have been said to posit a 'spiritual intelligence' though I have never done so, and have in fact explicitly rejected that possibility both orally and in writings" (p. 2). In an article the previous year Gardner (1995) asked whether it is appropriate to add spirituality to the list of intelligences deserves discussion and study in nonfringe psychological circles. In Gardner's (1997) book *Extraordinary Minds*, he devoted sections to "Spiritual Extraordinariness" and "Moral Extraordinariness." He noted several examples of the powerful influence that charismatic spiritual leaders (e.g., Pope John XXIII, Mahatma Gandhi, Martin Luther King, Jr.) can have on others, as well as extraordinary moral exemplars who sacrifice personal goals at great costs to themselves for broader, noble purposes.

Does spirituality meet Gardner's (1993) criteria for an intelligence? It may be useful to think of spirituality, in addition to the other meanings it took on, as comprised of a set of specific abilities or capacities. Spirituality may be then conceptualized in adaptive, cognitive–motivational terms, and, as such, may underlie a variety of problem-solving skills relevant to everyday life situations. This pragmatic approach to spirituality offers a perspective on spirituality that can counter the mistaken belief that spiritual states of mind are somehow on another "plane of existence"—a state of being that is phenomenologically valid, but has little relevance for problem solving and goal attainment in concrete life situations.

Before continuing this line of reasoning, however, a cautionary flag must be lifted. I do not wish to be misunderstood on the following important point. Viewing spirituality as an intelligence does not imply that spirituality is nothing more than problem solving, or that individuals merely "use" their spirituality to negotiate the problems of daily living. To make this erroneous inferential leap would be an example of committing the "nothing-but fallacy" (Paloutzian, 1996) which led to much misunderstanding in the psychology of religion. Spirituality is an enormously rich and diverse construct that defies easy definition, simple measurement, or easy identification in the life of another person. My thesis is twofold: (a) that there exist a set of skills and abilities associated with spirituality which are relevant to intelligence, and (b) individual differences in these skills constitute core features of the person. I am not suggesting that spirituality can be reduced to intelligence, or even to a set of cognitive abilities and capacities. I am not denying that there is a nonfunctional quality to faith that is not explicable in purely utilitarian terms.

Spirituality as a Knowledge Base

An *expert knowledge base* is a collection of information within a particular substantive realm that facilitates adaptation to the environment. Spiritual intelligence consists of a number of abilities and competencies that may be part of a person's expert knowledge. Spiritual information is part of a person's knowledge base that can lead to adaptive problem-solving behavior. For example, spiritual formation is precisely about building an expert knowledge base of information related to the sacred. Spirituality can serve as a source of information to individuals, and, as a function of interests and aptitudes, individuals become more or less skilled at processing this information. Through, for example, the study of sacred texts and the practice of spiritual exercises, depth and breadth of a spiritual knowledge base is developed and refined. Religions have been described as systems of information (Bowker, 1976; Hefner, 1993), providing individuals with resources that are essential for living a good life. Similarly, Mayer and Mitchell (1997) depicted religion as an emotion-based rule system that provides a context or backdrop for the generation of solutions to life problems, particularly those in the moral realm.

The Components of Spiritual Intelligence

There are at least five core abilities that define spiritual intelligence. These abilities have been valued if not in every known culture, then in the majority of cultures. Some cultures will place greater premium on some skills than on others (Kwilecki, 1988). There is nothing sacred about these five (in the sense that there are five and only five), nor do I present them in any predetermined order. At a minimum, spiritually intelligent individuals are characterized by (a) the capacity for transcendence; (b) the ability to enter into heightened spiritual states of consciousness; (c) the ability to invest everyday activities, events, and relationships with a sense of the sacred; (d) the ability to utilize spiritual resources to solve problems in living; and (e) the capacity to engage in virtuous behavior or to be virtuous (to show forgiveness, to express gratitude, to be humble, to display compassion). These five core components, representing individual differences in spiritual personality characteristics, are shown in Table 1.

Transcendence and mysticism.   The first two core components of spiritual intelligence deal with the capacity of the person to engage in heightened or extraordinary forms of consciousness. Transcendence connotes a rising above or going beyond the ordinary limits of physicality. It may describe rising above our natural world to relate with a divine being, or it may refer to going beyond our physical state to effect a heightened awareness of ourselves (Slife, Hope, & Nebeker, 1997). Themes of transcendence figure prominently in definitions of spirituality. For example, Elkins, Hedstrom, Hughes, Leaf, and Saunders (1988) stated that spirituality is "a way of being and experiencing that comes about through awareness of a transcendent dimension and that is characterized by certain identifiable values in regard to self, others, nature, life, and whatever one considers to be the Ultimate" (p. 10). Transcendence has been described as a fundamental capacity of persons that enables a person to sense a synchronicity to life and to develop a bond with humanity that cannot be severed, even by death (Piedmont, 1999). It has been viewed "as an art" capable of developing capacities of the mind such as attentional training and refining awareness (Walsh & Vaughan, 1993).

Mysticism is the awareness of an ultimate reality that takes the form of a sense of oneness or unity in which all boundaries disappear and objects are unified into a totality. Consider Shulman's (1995) description of a mystical experience that occurred while she was on a New York City subway train:

Suddenly the dull light in the car began to shine with exceptional lucidity until everything around me was glowing with an indescribable aura, and I saw in the row of mot-

TABLE 1
Core Components of Spiritual Intelligence

1. The capacity to transcend the physical and material.
2. The ability to experience heightened states of consciousness.
3. The ability to sanctify everyday experience.
4. The ability to utilize spiritual resources to solve problems.
5. The capacity to be virtuous.

ley passengers opposite the miraculous connection of all living beings. Not felt; saw. What began as a desultory thought grew to a vision, large and unifying, in which all the people in the car hurtling downtown together, like all the people on the planet hurtling together around the sun—our entire living cohort—formed one united family, indissolubly connected by the rare and mysterious accident of life. No matter what our countless superficial differences, we were equal, we were one, by virtue of simply being alive at this moment out of all of the possible moments stretching endlessly back and ahead. The vision filled me with an overwhelming love for the entire human race and a feeling that no matter how incomplete or damaged our lives, we were surpassingly lucky to be alive. (pp. 55–56)

Spiritually intelligent individuals are likely to be especially skilled in entering these states of consciousness, as well as other spiritual states, such as contemplative prayer (Foster, 1992). Considerable empirical work has been conducted on mystical experience (see Hood, Spilka, Gorsuch, & Hunsberger, 1996, chap. 6–7 for a review). Newberg and d'Aquili (1998) described the social significance of unitary spiritual experiences arising from ceremonial religious rituals as well as the physiological benefits from individual meditation.

Sanctification.   Sanctification encapsulates the third component of spiritual intelligence. To *sanctify* means to set apart for a special purpose—for a holy or a godly purpose. A recognition of the presence of the divine in ordinary activities is an aspect of spiritual knowing in all major religions of the world (Monk et al., 1998). Contemporary research is documenting that there are important consequences of this sanctification process. When work is seen as a calling rather than a job (Davidson & Caddell, 1994; Novak, 1996), or when parenting is viewed as a sacred responsibility (Dollahite, 1998), it is likely to be approached differently than when viewed in purely secular terms. Even seemingly ordinary activities such as running or golf can become imbued with spiritual significance (Murphy, 1972). In the film *Chariots of Fire* (Hudson, 1981), Eric Liddell reflects on the deeper significance of running in revealing that "when I run, I feel His pleasure." Religious sanctification occurs when the self, family, home, occupation, and goals are imbued with the sacred. Mahoney et al. (1999) found that when marital partners viewed their relationship as imbued with divine qualities, they reported greater levels of marital satisfaction, more constructive problem-solving behaviors, decreased marital conflict, and greater commitment to the relationship compared to couples who did not see their marriage in a sacred light.

Casting in the language of intelligence enables sanctification to be viewed as expertise that people might bring to bear to solve problems and plan effective action. Emmons, Cheung, and Tehrani (1998) demonstrated that personal strivings in life can become spiritualized through a process of sanctification. *Spiritual strivings* are intentional states that represent ultimate concerns in a person's life. Imbued with a sense of the sacred, these goals take on a significance and power not found in secular strivings (Emmons et al., 1998). Drawing on Tillich's (1957) conception of religion as ultimate concern described in the beginning of this article, Emmons et al. (1998) developed criteria for reliably identifying ultimate concerns through personal goal strivings. Examples of spiritual strivings are "discern God's will for my life," "apply knowledge of the Koran to everyday life," "be compassionate and forgiving," "lovingly share the gospel with my coworkers," and "focus my life so that I might get closer to God." Research indicates that when people's lives are oriented around ultimate concerns, they tend to experience a sense of meaningfulness, fulfillment, and personality unification (Emmons, 1999; Emmons et al., 1998).

Religious and spiritual coping. The fourth characteristic, the ability to utilize spiritual resources to solve problems in living, encompasses religious and spiritual coping (Pargament, 1997). Pargament reviews a large literature documenting the effectiveness of spiritual and religious resources in the coping process. Problem solving is the *sine qua non* of effective coping, as effective coping entails the implementation of problem-solving skills. Lazarus and Folkman (1984) defined problem solving as

the ability to search for information, analyze situations for the purpose of identifying the problem in order to generate alternative courses of action, weigh alternative courses of action, weigh alternatives with respect to desired or anticipated outcomes, and select and implement an appropriate plan of action. (p. 162)

These are abilities that are required when prior goals are abandoned and new goals are adopted. Spiritual conversions can shape the reprioritization of goals (Paloutzian, Richardson, & Rambo, 1999), and the ability to revise and reprioritize goals are indicators of intelligence (Haslam & Baron, 1994). Furthermore, intrinsically religious individuals are more likely to be adept at handling traumatically induced stress; they are more likely to find meaning in traumatic crises and are more likely to experience growth following trauma than are less religious persons (Park, Cohen, & Murch, 1996). Not all forms of spiritual coping are equally effective; for example, collaboration with God is generally more adaptive than is passively deferring to God (Pargament, 1997).

Virtuous traits. The fifth and final component of spiritual intelligence is reflected in the capacity to engage in virtuous behavior on a consistent basis: to show forgiveness, to express gratitude, to exhibit humility, to be compassionate, and to display sacrificial love. There is no pretense here that this list is exhaustive. These virtues are included under the rubric of spiritual intelligence because of the salience of these concepts in virtually all major religious traditions. They are considered skills in that from Aristotle to the present (Wallace, 1978; Zagzebski, 1996) these qualities are seen as capable of being cultivated through practice and instruction. Zagzebski (1996) defines virtues as "acquired excellences of the person," coming closer to "defining who the person is than any other category of qualities" (p. 135).

Virtues connect to both motivation, representing ultimate concerns, and to effective action. Conceiving of these inner qualities as virtues, implies that these are sources of human strength that enable people to function effectively in the world. Of longstanding interest to moral philosophers (Zagzebski, 1996) and theologians (Schimmel, 1997), psychologists are beginning to turn their attention to the study of these human strengths (Baumeister & Exline, 1999; Seligman, 1998). Baumeister and Exline (1999) proposed that self-control is the core psychological trait underlying the majority of virtues, and is essential for success in virtually all life domains. Similarly, self-control failures lie at the heart of the seven deadly sins: gluttony, sloth, pride, anger, greed, lust, and envy. In a later section, I elaborate on the benefits of one virtue in particular, humility.

Identifying these core components is the starting point for postulating a construct of spiritual intelligence. Whether there are more or less than these five characteristics is open for debate. At this early stage of development, the study of spiritual intelligence can most benefit from a broad conceptual approach. As more is learned about spiritual traits and skills through scientific research, more definitive statements concerning these core capacities will be possible. In the meantime, I believe that each of these five are justifiable aspects of a broader capacity that might be called spiritual intelligence. The framework is also falsifiable. Should research demonstrate that the core abilities do not cluster together, the higher order nature of the spiritual intelligence construct would be called into question.

Does Spirituality Fit Gardner's Criteria?

Postulating spirituality as a set of related abilities and competencies is the first step for qualifying it as a form of intelligence, but we have yet to see how it stacks up against the accepted MI theory. Does spirituality pass the test for an intelligence? Meeting the criteria that Gardner (1993) proposed requires marshaling neurological, developmental, evolutionary, and psychological evidence. Relevant data from each of these sources are becoming available. What follows is an illustration from each of these areas. I have already presented what I believe constitute the core abilities involved in this type of intelligence (Criteria 1). As Gardner's approach is based largely on brain function, I begin with the biological level of analysis. Other theories of intelligence propose somewhat alternative criteria for the establishment of an intelligence (e.g., Sternberg, 1997). For the reasons described earlier, I have chosen Gardner's theory as a benchmark.

Evolutionary plausibility.   The biological basis of spirituality and religious-ness can be examined at three levels of analysis: evolutionary biology, behavior ge-netics, and neural systems. Arguments for the evolutionary plausibility of religion have come from a number of different quarters—from biologists, psychologists, anthropologists, and theologians (Hood, Spilka, Hunsberger, & Gorsuch, 1996; Kirkpatrick, 1999; McClennon, 1997; Pinker, 1997; Wilson, 1978). From a psy-chological perspective, evolutionary biology has been proposed as providing an in-tegrative framework for religious beliefs, practices, and commitments (Kirkpatrick, 1999). Kirkpatrick contended that the universal success of religious belief systems is attributable to religion tapping into a broad array of psychological mechanisms that evolved via natural selection to solve a specific class of problems faced by our ancestors. Furthermore, these mechanisms exist at both the cultural level, expressed through corporate religion, and at the level of individual, in terms of personal religiousness or spirituality. Kirkpatrick discussed a variety of evolved mechanisms that underlie a variety of religious beliefs and behaviors, including at-tachment, coalition formation, social exchange, kin-based altruism, and mate selection.

Behavior genetic studies.   Evidence for the heritability of religious atti-tudes suggests genetic influence (D'Onofrio, Eaves, Murrelle, Maes, & Spilka, 1999; Waller, Kojetin, Bouchard, Lykken, & Tellegen, 1990). D'Onofrio et al. amassed an impressive database that enabled them to explore the intergenerational transmission of religious attitudes and behaviors. They found evidence that whereas religious affiliation is primarily determined by shared fam-ily environment, religious attitudes (primarily religious conservatism) and be-haviors are moderately influenced by genetic factors. The heritability estimates for religiousness are on the magnitude of that which is typically seen for personal-ity traits.

Whether the core elements of what I am calling spiritual intelligence have a significant genetic component remains to be determined. However, given pre-liminary data from the field of behavior genetics on the heritability of religious-ness, it would be surprising if spiritual intelligence turned out to be unrelated to genetic factors. There may also be implications of such a genetic link for inter-personal problem solving. In the largest study on personality and divorce under-taken, Jockin, McGue, and Lykken (1996) found that of 11 personality traits, traditionalism was the strongest negative predictor of divorce risk. Traditional-ism correlates about .5 with measures of religious commitment (Lykken & Tellegen, 1996) and is also highly heritable (Tellegen et al., 1988). Jockin et al. suggested that personality acts as a conduit of genetic influence on divorce risk, harkening back to Mahoney et al.'s (1999) finding that marital satisfaction is as-sociated with constructive problem solving.

Neurobiology of spiritual experience.   The heritability of aspects of religiousness points to the role of biology, but is unable to specify relevant neural mechanisms. The growing field of neuroscience is also contributing to an understanding of the biological basis of spirituality in a way that might elucidate neural substrates. Recall that Gardner (1993) believed that specific brain structures underlie different types of intelligences, and that a given intelligence should be isolable by studying brain-damaged patients. Brain scientists have begun to investigate the neural bases of religious and spiritual experience, both in terms of neural substrates of religious experience and their alteration in brain dysfunctions (Brown, 1998; Jeeves, 1998; Saver & Rabin, 1997). Neuroscience research demonstrates that there may exist distinctive neurobiological systems (primarily in the limbic regions) for religious experience, particularly for the mystical experiences of oneness and unity (d'Aquili & Newberg, 1998; Newberg & d'Aquili, 1999). Although the exact nature of these mechanisms is not uncontroversial the discovery of these systems strengthens the case for spirituality as an intelligence.

Psychometric evidence.   Yet another of Gardner's (1993) criteria for the existence of an intelligence is support from psychometric findings. Inventories to measure spiritual and religious states have proliferated at an alarming rate in recent years. Some have even called for a moratorium on the construction of new measures (Gorsuch, 1984). Piedmont (1999) presented data on the independence of spiritual transcendence from the five-factor model of personality, suggesting that spirituality may represent a heretofore unacknowledged sixth major dimension of personality. Furthermore, psychometric investigations have revealed that measures of spiritual transcendence and religious attitudes are statistically independent of measures of general intelligence (Francis, 1998; Piedmont, 1999).

There exists no measure of spiritual intelligence, per se. I am skeptical that an adequate self-report measure could be easily constructed; on the contrary, it would be quite ill-advised to attempt to gauge someone's "spiritual IQ." Ability-based measures would be more promising, following the lead of Mayer, Caruso, and Salovey (in press). A consensus on the scientific viability of the construct must first be established, although, before measurement efforts are undertaken.

A characteristic developmental history.   An intelligence should show a definable developmental history. Spirituality would appear to meet this criterion (Fowler, 1981; Kwilecki, 1988; Levenson & Crumpler, 1996). Stage-centered models of faith development propose that there are universal stages that characterize spiritual growth and the capacity to engage in spiritual ways of knowing. Adult spiritual development has become an area of vigorous theory and research in recent years (Weibust & Thomas, 1996). That there is an age-related readiness to perceiving transcendent truths is less controversial in comparison to the disagreement that exists over whether such spiritual development is generalistic versus particularistic (Kwilecki, 1988; McFadden, 1999; Wulff, 1997). There are differing levels of expertise or sophistication in spiritual abilities, from novitiate to expert, as there are in other systems of knowledge (Gardner, 1997).

Susceptibility to encoding in symbol system.   Yet another criterion for an intelligence is susceptibility to encoding in a symbol system (Gardner, 1993; May, 1960; Monk et al., 1998; Tillich, 1957). This criterion is not likely to be controversial. Symbol systems have always played a major role in religious traditions to express truths and insights not reducible to linguistic expression. Religious symbols serve the function of enabling people to grasp a transcendent, ultimate reality within a shared community of believers; hence symbols are socially constructed. Religious symbols "have a power that distinguish them from other symbols; they deal with issues that are the deepest of all concerns a human may have, with ultimate meaning" (Monk et al., 1998, p. 79). Gardner (1993) considered rituals, religious codes, and mythic and totemic systems as symbolic codes that "capture and convey crucial aspects of personal intelligence" (p. 242).

Exemplars of spiritual intelligence.   The existence of spiritually exceptional individuals (the Catholic mystics St. Theresa of Avila and St. John of the Cross, and the Sufi master Ibn 'Arabi are three excellent examples) can be taken as evidence that spiritual skills are highly developed in certain individuals (Gardner, 1997). If we examine individuals considered to be spiritually exceptional, we can see how well the concept of spiritual intelligence fits. Consider, for example, the 12th-century Sufi master Ibn 'Arabi (Nasr, 1964). Ibn 'Arabi was well known for his capacity for transcendence and his ability to enter into heightened spiritual states of consciousness, and is known to be among the most prolific of Islamic mystical writers, listing at least 250 titles. It is clear from his writings that they were not merely the result of long mental and intellectual deliberations, but were also drawn from mystical visions and experiences. Ibn 'Arabi acknowledged that much of what he wrote came to him in mystical visions, while asleep and as direct revelation from God.

Although well known as a spiritual master and teacher, Ibn 'Arabi was also quite capable of applying his spirituality to everyday life. At the early age of 20, he married, was employed as Secretary to the Governor of Seville, and spent much of his life in the formal study of politics, religion, and science. A strong advocate of the necessity of law and formal doctrine for the good of the community, he strictly applied this in his advice to political leaders. Yet, at an early age he astounded his teachers and many influential leaders in his country (e.g., the philosopher

Averroes) with his insightful views of mystical transcendence and how to integrate spirituality within one's life.

Ibn 'Arabi devoted the majority of his life to the study of mystical doctrine and experience and remained quite humble, compassionate, and virtuous. Well known and sought after as a spiritual master, his report of a particular incident while teaching gives insight into his character. Ibn 'Arabi reported,

> their respect for me prevented them from being relaxed, and they were all very correct and silent; so I sought a means of making them more relaxed saying to my host, 'May I bring your attention to a composition of mine entitled *Guidance in Flouting the Usual Courtesies*, and expound a chapter from it to you?' He answered that he would very much like to hear it. I then pushed my foot into his lap and told him to massage it, whereupon they understood my meaning and behaved in a more relaxed manner. (Austin, 1980, pp. 5–6)

Summary.   To summarize, converging lines of evidence appear to support the thesis that spirituality does, in fact, meet several of the acceptable criteria for an intelligence. But does spirituality foster adaptive functioning in daily life? Recall that most of the definitions stated earlier that intelligence, particularly practical forms of intelligence, is reflected in effectiveness in life. Is there evidence that spiritual states facilitate performance in important life domains? Conversely, does an absence of spiritual intelligence portend dysfunction?

The Adaptiveness of Spiritual Intelligence: Humility as an Example

At the conclusion of his book on experiential intelligence, Epstein (1993) closed by invoking spirituality as a pathway to the higher reaches of the experiential mind:

> The beacon for the spiritual path is faith in some power or force that transcends ordinary human understanding. Such faith is the source of a broad perspective and a feeling of connectedness with a greater whole than exists in one's immediate experience.... This deep spiritual identification which transcends rational calculation, enables people to take the long view and experience its ultimate consequences without effort ... at this, its highest level of functioning, the experiential mind becomes not a betrayer of long-range interests and concern for others, but a means for their achievement. (p. 267)

Epstein voiced faith in the adaptiveness of a transcendent, spiritual orientation to the world. What is the evidence for the adaptiveness of the spiritual abilities and competencies that comprise spiritual intelligence? There is growing evidence that spiritually oriented lifestyles tend to protect people from unintelligent behavior; for example, from engaging in personally and societally destructive ways (Paloutzian & Kirkpatrick, 1995). There are certainly counterexamples; for instance, the ascetics who engage in "holy anorexia" (Wulff, 1997). At this point, however, I would like to discuss an element of spiritual intelligence that in particular appears to enable effective functioning, one that has not received much attention in psychology, humility.

Although humility is often equated with low self-regard, humility appears to be a source of human strength. *Humility* is the realistic appraisal of one's strengths and weaknesses—neither overestimating nor underestimating them. To be humble is not to have a low opinion of oneself, it is to have an accurate opinion of oneself. It is the ability to keep one's talents and accomplishments in perspective (Richards, 1992), to have a sense of self-acceptance, an understanding of one's imperfections, and to be free from arrogance and low self-esteem (Clark, 1992). In most philosophical treatments, humility is considered a virtue—a desirable characteristic to cultivate. History is replete with humble exemplars—powerful spiritual, political, and scientific leaders who were characterized by a sense of perspective about their goals and themselves, refusing to succumb to the temptation of self-aggrandizement.

Humility has been linked to a number of personal and interpersonal life outcomes. In the health field, research reported that a lack of humility—or the excessive self-focus found in the trait of narcissism—is a risk factor for coronary heart disease (Bracke & Thoresen, 1996; Scherwitz & Canick, 1988). Another study found that narcissism in ex-spouses was a strong predictor of continued conflict between them, with destructive consequences for their children (Ehrenberg, Hunter, & Elterman, 1996). Earlier we saw that informational search is part and parcel of problem solving. Humility has been associated with better informational search abilities and problem-solving efficiency (Weiss & Knight, 1980), and with ratings of teaching effectiveness (Bridges, Ware, Brown, & Greenwood, 1971). Humility is also strongly linked with morality. Humility was one criterion that Colby and Damon (1992) used for identifying moral excellence in their in-depth study of moral exemplars. Thus, humility appears to facilitate success in a wide range of life endeavors, and is an example of the adaptiveness of one aspect of spiritual intelligence.

One other example of the adaptiveness of spirituality can be briefly noted. Sacks (1979) examined the effect of spiritual exercises on integration of the self-concept. In a sample of 50 Jesuit novices, he found that a 4-week period of secluded meditation resulted in a significant increase in self-integration, as measured by Loevinger's concept of ego development. Although no long-term follow-up was available the 30-day exercise apparently increased these men's ability to assimilate conflicting self-representations into a unified self-system. Successful self-regulation requires the effective management of systemic goal conflict, a skill which seems to be facilitated by spiritual practices and spiritual strivings (Emmons et al., 1998).

IS THERE AN OPTIMAL LEVEL OF SPIRITUAL INTELLIGENCE?

Spiritual intelligence has been conceived of in this article as largely a positive construct. There are benefits to being spiritually intelligent, just as there are benefits to any form of intelligence. Yet, can one have too much of a good thing? Is there a down side to being spiritually intelligent? Is there an optimal amount of spiritual intelligence? Or to phrase the question differently, does it make sense to describe someone as "spiritually unintelligent?" These are intriguing and vital questions to ponder. That there is a dark side to the religious life is beyond question. The construct of spiritual intelligence may be able to shed light on the possible harmfulness of religious beliefs or spiritually oriented lifestyles. As with other skills, spiritual intelligence may be put to nefarious as well as to noble ends. It is not inevitably a positive attribute.

It is evident that a person could overdevelop his or her spiritual intellect while ignoring other areas of functioning. There is a danger in becoming spiritual to the point that one is unable to act effectively in the world, for instance, being so "otherworldly focused" that one is unable to function effectively with the concrete demands of daily life. A spiritually intelligent person is able to harmonize earthly and heavenly spirituality.

Problems in psychological or interpersonal functioning might stem from an imbalance in the development of the specific components, or with an exclusive concern with some components to the neglect of others. For example, there may be individuals who have highly developed capacities for transcendence or mystical experiences, yet who have lived a life of passive detachment from this world. Conversely, there may be disadvantages to being too easily forgiving, too grateful, too humble, or too self-controlled. Perhaps extremes in each of the components may become maladaptive, particularly when combined with emotional instability, basic character flaws, or an inability to channel one's spiritual intellegence in a noble direction.

Advantages of Linking Spirituality with Intelligence

Viewing spirituality as a type of intelligence enlarges the concept of spirituality to encompass meanings not typically associated with it. Spiritual intelligence enhances the plausibility of a scientific spirituality by locating spirituality within an existing acceptable psychological framework, one that proved to be extremely useful in understanding the common ground between personality and behavior. It allows spirituality to become anchored to rational approaches to the mind that emphasize goal attainment and problem solving (Haslam & Baron, 1994; Pinker, 1997). Moreover, the spiritual intelligence framework opens the door for new links to be forged with areas of psychology that have been slow to examine spiritual issues, including developmental, cognitive, and much of personality psychology. Conversely, an anchoring of spirituality in the intelligence tradition might enable theology to deal with challenges that arise from cognitive science and other naturalistic frameworks that attempt to model human nature (Brand, 1997; Peterson, 1997).

Antidote for Antireligious Intellectualism

Religion and intelligence are two words that are not often used together. Linking spirituality with intelligence can provide an antidote for antireligious intellectualism (Marsden, 1997) in which religious and spiritual world views are seen as irrational, emotional, and illogical, akin to superstitious thinking. Arguing from a similar perspective in their theory of emotional intelligence, Mayer and Salovey (1997) began with the premise that emotions and intelligence are often viewed as incompatible because the former are perceived as an "intrinsically irrational and disruptive force" (p. 9). Instead of dichotonizing faith and reason, this way of thinking about spirituality recognizes that spiritual processing can contribute to effective cognitive functioning rather than preclude it.

An Integrative Framework for Spirituality and Health

Spiritual intelligence also provides an integrative framework for understanding the salutary effects of religion on psychological, physical, and interpersonal outcomes. Spirituality is a predictor of adherence to health care regimens (Fox, Pitkin, Paul, Carson, & Duan, 1998; Naguib, Geiser, & Comstock, 1968; O'Brien, 1982) and adherence is generally intelligent (see Karoly, 1994, for application of an intelligence framework to the study of medical adherence). The intelligent use of spiritual information can contribute to positive life outcomes such as emotional well-being, positive social functioning, and an enhanced overall quality of life. Each of these domains of functioning would appear to benefit from exercise of the spiritual intellect.

Spirituality as a Dynamic Construct

In defining and measuring spirituality or religiousness, it is all too easy to conceive spiritual and religious variables as passive, static trait-like entities. Spirituality and religiousness become something that a person has or possesses (e.g., beliefs), or behaviors that are engaged in (rituals). Alternatively, viewing spirituality as a set of skills, resources, capacities, or abilities enables spirituality to take on active, dynamic properties. Spirituality not only *is* something, it *does* something. As a dynamic property of persons, spiritual intelligence provides an interpretive context for negotiating demands of daily life.

Increased Appreciation for Cross-Cultural Expressions of Spirituality

As with other intelligences, spiritual intelligence includes abilities and competencies that are differentially valued in different cultures. Yang and Sternberg (1997) described different conceptions of intelligence in Taoist and Confucianist Chinese cultures. Character virtues such as humility and benevolence play a much greater role in defining intelligence in these traditions than in contemporary Western views of intelligence. Notions of wisdom, morality, and intelligence are virtually inseparable in Chinese religious systems. Tethering spirituality and intelligence enables an acknowledgment of and deeper appreciation for spiritual and religious ways of knowing that might be highly prized in certain cultures.

Cultivation of Spiritual Skills

Postulating spiritual competencies and abilities to be relatively independent human faculties opens the door to the possibility that they can be cultivated in a manner analogous to other types of intelligences. Gardner (1993) argued that communities selectively identify particular competencies for development and elaboration. If spiritual intelligence does indeed confer individual and societal advantages, if the world would be a better place if people were more "spiritually intelligent," the desirability and feasibility of strategic efforts to augment it ought to be investigated. Just as educational programs have been developed to teach emotional skills (Salovey & Sluyter, 1997), spiritual skills could similarly be acquired and cultivated. After all, the purpose of character education programs (Lickona, 1991) is to foster spiritual virtues and spiritual maturity so as to produce productive and socially responsible members of society. A spiritually intelligent character education program would go beyond the teaching of socioemotional skills to include the basic spiritual competencies and abilities described in this article. For example, Lickona discussed how humility is an essential component of good character. It is also one of the components of spiritual intelligence, and as we saw earlier, is predictive of a variety of positive life outcomes.

CONCLUSIONS

My goal in this article was to introduce into scientific discourse the concept of spiritual intelligence, to review the evidence for spirituality as a set of related competencies, and to examine how spirituality fares when standard criteria for evaluating an intelligence are applied. It would be premature at this point to argue that the existence of a spiritual intelligence was incontrovertibly demonstrated. Yet, spirituality did appear to meet virtually all of the criteria as specified by Gardner's (1993) theory of MI. According to Mayer et al. (in press), intelligences that are valid according to MI criteria are "definitely worth studying and may provide information for the next generation of intelligence tests" (p. 22).

Spiritual intelligence suggests new domains of intelligent action in the world. Abilities in the spiritual realm are a significant aspect of what it means to be an intelligent, rational, and purposeful human being, striving to align one's life with the Ultimate. There are many ways to be intelligent, yet spirituality has not been studied within mainstream research on intelligence and personality. Psychologists continue to divide and subdivide intelligence in many ways, but absent from such partitioning is a spiritual or religious way of knowing. Conversely, the potential explanatory and integrative force that intelligence can provide has been neglected by psychologists interested in religious and spiritual issues. An intelligence-based conception of spirituality can stimulate progress in the psychology of religion and can be determinative of future theoretical and research agendas. Hood, Spilka, Hunsberger, and Gorsuch (1996) encouraged researchers to examine constructs that originally derived their meaning from within religious traditions, in order to "enliven the psychology of religion" (p. 198). Spiritual intelligence may be one such enlivening construct. Its status as a meaningful scientific construct will require additional conceptualization, research, and debate in scientific circles.

ACKNOWLEDGMENTS

I am grateful to Stacey Anderson, Warren Brown, Cheryl Crumpler, Seymour Epstein, Rick Levenson, Jack Mayer, Ray Paloutzian, Ken Pargament, and Jefferson Singer for their insightful and encouraging comments on an earlier version of this article. I also thank the following individuals who were kind enough to share with me their thoughts about spiritual intelligence: David Wulff, Sherwood Lingenfelter, T. George Harris, Newton Malony, Dave Dollahite, and Bob Wheeler.

REFERENCES

Allport, G. W. (1950). *The individual and his religion.* New York: Macmillan.

Apter, M. J. (1985). Religious states of mind: A reversal theory interpretation. In L. B. Brown (Ed.), *Advances in the psychology of religion* (pp. 62–75). Oxford, NY: Pergamon.

Austin, R. W. J. (1980). *Ibn Al-'Arabi: The bezels of wisdom.* New York: Paulist Press.

Baumeister, R. F., & Exline, J. J. (1999). Virtue, personality, and social relations: Self-control as the moral muscle. *Journal of Personality, 67,* 1165–1194.

Bowker, J. W. (1976). Information process, systems behavior, and the study of religion. *Zygon, 11,* 361–379.

Bracke, P. E., & Thoresen, C. E. (1996). Reducing Type A behavior patterns: A structured-group approach. In R. Allan & S. S. Scheidt (Eds.), *Heart & mind: The practice of cardiac psychology* (pp. 255–290). Washington, DC: American Psychological Association.

Brand, J. L. (1997). Challenges for a Christian psychology from cognitive science. *Journal of Psychology and Christianity, 16,* 233–246.

Bregman, L., & Thierman, S. (1995). *First person mortal: Personal narratives of illness, dying, and grief.* New York: Paragon.

Bridges, C. M., Ware, W. B., Brown, B. B., & Greenwood, G. (1971). Characteristics of the best and worst college teachers. *Science Education, 55,* 545–553.

Brown, W. S. (1998). Cognitive contributions to soul. In N. Murphy & W. S. Brown (Eds.), *Portraits of human nature* (pp. 99–125). Minneapolis, MN: Fortress.

Chiu, C., Hong, Y., & Dweck, C. S. (1994). Toward an integrative model of personality and intelligence: A general framework and some preliminary steps. In R. J. Sternberg & P. Ruzgis (Eds.), *Personality and intelligence* (pp. 104–134). New York: Cambridge University Press.

Clark, A. T. (1992). Humility. In D. H. Ludlow (Ed.), *Encyclopedia of Mormonism* (pp. 663–664). New York: Macmillan.

Colby, A., & Damon, W. (1992). *Some do care: Contemporary lives of moral commitment.* New York: Free Press.

d'Aquili, E. G., & Newberg, A. B. (1998). The neuropsychological basis of religion, or why God won't go away. *Zygon, 33,* 187–202.

Davidson, J. C., & Caddell, D. P. (1994). Religion and the meaning of work. *Journal for the Scientific Study of Religion, 33,* 135–147.

Dollahite, D. C. (1998). Faith, fathering, and spirituality. *The Journal of Men's Studies, 7,* 3–15.

D'Onofrio, B. M., Eaves, L. J., Murrelle, L., Maes, H. H., & Spilka, B. (1999). Understanding biological and social influences on religious affiliation, attitudes, and behaviors: A behavior–genetic perspective. *Journal of Personality, 67,* 953–984.

Dweck, C. S. (1990). Self-theories and goals: Their role in motivation, personality, and development. *Nebraska Symposium on Motivation* (pp. 199–235). Lincoln: University of Nebraska Press.

Ehrenberg, M. F., Hunter, M. A., & Elterman, M. F. (1996). Shared parenting agreements after marital separation: The roles of empathy and narcissism. *Journal of Consulting and Clinical Psychology, 64,* 808–818.

Elkins, D. N., Hedstrom, L. J., Hughes, L. L., Leaf, J. A., & Saunders, C. (1988). Towards a humanistic–phenomenological spirituality: Definition, description, and measurement. *Journal of Humanistic Psychology, 28,* 5–18.

Emmons, R. A. (1986). Personal strivings: An approach to personality and subjective well-being. *Journal of Personality and Social Psychology, 51,* 1058–1068.

Emmons, R. A. (1999). *The psychology of ultimate concerns: Motivation and spirituality in personality.* New York: Guilford.

Emmons, R. A., Cheung, C., & Tehrani, K. (1998). Assessing spirituality through personal goals: Implications for research on religion and subjective well-being. *Social Indicators Research, 45,* 391–422.

Emmons, R. A., & King, L. A. (1988). Conflict among personal strivings: Immediate and long-term implications for psychological and physical well-being. *Journal of Personality and Social Psychology, 54,* 1040–1048.

Epstein, S. (1993). *You're smarter than you think: How to develop your practical intelligence for success in living.* New York: Simon & Schuster.

Ford, M. E. (1994). A living systems approach to the integration of personality and intelligence. In R. J. Sternberg & P. Ruzgis (Eds.), *Personality and intelligence* (pp. 188–217). New York: Cambridge University Press.

Foster, R. J. (1992). *Prayer: Finding the heart's true home.* San Francisco: HarperCollins.

Fowler, J. W. (1981). *Stages of faith: The psychology of human development and the quest for meaning.* New York: HarperCollins.

Fox, S. A., Pitkin, K., Paul, C., Carson, S., & Duan, N. (1998). Breast cancer screening adherence: Does church attendance matter? *Health Education and Behavior, 25,* 742–758.

Francis, L. J. (1998). The relationship between intelligence and religiosity among 15–16 year-olds. *Mental Health, Religion, & Culture, 1,* 185–196.

Gardner, H. (1993). *Frames of mind: The theory of multiple intelligences.* New York: Basic Books.

Gardner, H. (1995, November). Reflections on multiple intelligences: Myths and messages. *Phi Delta Kappan,* 204–207.

Gardner, H. (1996, November). Probing more deeply into the theory of multiple intelligences. *NASSP Bulletin,* 1–7.

Gardner, H. (1997). *Extraordinary minds.* New York: Basic Books.

Gorsuch, R. L. (1984). Measurement: The boon and bane of investigating religion. *American Psychologist, 39,* 228–236.

Haslam, N., & Baron, J. (1994). Intelligence, prudence, and personality. In R. J. Sternberg & P. Ruzgis (Eds.), *Personality and intelligence* (pp. 32–58). New York: Cambridge University Press.

Hefner, P. (1993). *The human factor.* Minneapolis, MN: Fortress.

Heschel, A. (1955). *God in search of man: A philosophy of Judaism.* New York: Farrar, Straus & Cudahy.

Hood, R. W., Jr., Spilka. B., Gorsuch. R., & Hunsberger, B. (1996). *The psychology of religion: An empirical approach* (2nd ed.). New York: Guilford.

Hudson, H. (Director). (1981). *Chariots of fire.* [Film]. (Available from Warner Home Video)

Jeeves, M. A. (1998). Brain, mind, and behavior. In N. Murphy & W. S. Brown, (Eds.), *Portraits of human nature* (pp. 73–98). Minneapolis, MN: Fortress.

Jockin, V., McGue, M., & Lykken, D. T. (1996). Personality and divorce: A genetic analysis. *Journal of Personality and Social Psychology, 71,* 288–299.

Karoly, P. (1994). Enlarging the scope of the compliance construct: Toward developmental and motivational relevance. In N. A. Krasnegor, L. H. Epstein, S. B. Johnson, & S. J. Yaffe (Eds.), *Developmental aspects of health care compliance* (pp. 11–27). Hillsdale, NJ: Lawrence Erlbaum Associates, Inc.

Kirkpatrick, L. A. (1999). Toward an evolutionary psychology of religion and personality. *Journal of Personality, 67,* 921–952.

Kwilecki, S. (1988). A scientific approach to religious development: Proposals and a case illustration. *Journal for the Scientific Study of Religion, 27,* 307–325.

Lazarus, R. S., & Folkman, S. (1984). *Stress, appraisal, and coping.* New York: Springer.

Levenson, M. R., & Crumpler, C. (1996). Three models of adult development. *Human Development, 39,* 135–149.

Lickona, T. (1991). *Educating for character: How our schools can teach respect and responsibility.* New York: Bantam.

Lykken, D. T., & Tellegen, A. (1996). Happiness is a stochastic phenomenon. *Psychological Science, 7,* 186–189.

Mahoney, A., Pargament, K. I., Jewell, T., Swank. A. B., Scott, E., Emery, E., & Rye, M. (1999). Marriage and the spiritual realm: The roles of proximal and distal religious constructs in marital functioning. *Journal of Family Psychology, 13,* 321–338.

Marsden, G. M. (1997). *The outrageous idea of Christian scholarship.* New York: Oxford University Press.

May, R. (Ed.). (1960). *Symbolism in religion and literature.* New York: Braziller.

Mayer, J. D., Caruso, D., & Salovey, P. (in press). Competing models of emotional intelligence. In R. J. Sternberg (Ed.), *Handbook of human intelligence.* New York: Cambridge University Press.

Mayer, J. D., & Mitchell, D. C. (1997). Intelligence as a subsystem of personality: From Spearman's G to contemporary models of hot processsing. In W. Tomic & J. Kingma (Eds.), *Reflections on the concept of intelligence.* Greenwich, CT: JAI.

Mayer, J. D., & Salovey, P. (1997). What is emotional intelligence? In P. Salovey & D. J. Sluyter (Eds.), *Emotional development and emotional intelligence* (pp. 3–31). New York: Basic Books.

McClennon, J. (1997). Shamanic healing, human evolution, and the origin of religion. *Journal for the Scientific Study of Religion, 36,* 345–354.

McFadden, S. H. (1999). Religion, personality, and aging: A life span perspective. *Journal of Personality, 67,* 1081–1104.

Monk, R. C., Hofheinz, W. C., Lawrence, K. T., Stamey, J. D., Affleck, B., & Yamamori, T. (1998). *Exploring religious meaning* (5th ed.). Upper Saddle River, NJ: Prentice Hall.

Murphy, M. (1972). *Golf in the kingdom.* New York: Dell.

Naguib, S. M., Geiser, P. B., & Comstock, G. W. (1968). Responses to a program of screening for cervical cancer. *Public Health Reports, 83,* 990–998.

Nasr, S. (1964). Ibn 'Arabi and the Sufis. In *Three Muslim sages* (pp. 83–121). Cambridge, MA: Harvard University Press.

Neisser, U., Boodoo, G., Bouchard, T. T., Jr., Boykin, A. W., Brody, N., Ceci, S. J., Halpern, D. F., Loehlin, J. C., Perloff, R., Sternberg, R. J., & Urbina, A. (1996). Intelligence: Known and unknowns. *American Psychologist, 51,* 77–101.

Newberg, A. S., & d'Aquili, E. G. (1998). The neuropsychology of spiritual experience. In H. Koenig (Ed.), *Handbook of religion and mental health* (pp. 76–94). San Diego: Academic.

Novak, M. (1996). *Business as a calling: Work and the examined life.* New York: Free Press.

O'Brien, M. E. (1982). Religious faith and adjustment to long-term hemodialysis. *Journal of Religion and Health, 21,* 68–80.

Paloutzian, R. F. (1996). *Invitation to the psychology of religion* (2nd ed.). Boston: Allyn & Bacon.

Paloutzian, R. F., & Kirkpatrick, L. A. (1995). Introduction: The scope of religious influences on personal and societal well-being. *Journal of Social Issues, 51,* 1–11.

Paloutzian, R. F., Richardson, J. T., & Rambo, L. R. (1999). Religious conversion and personality change. *Journal of Personality, 67,* 1047–1079.

Pargament, K. I. (1997). *The psychology of religion and coping.* New York: Guilford.

Pargament, K. I., & Park, C. L. (1995). Merely a defense? The variety of religious means and ends. *Journal of Social Issues, 51,* 13–32.

Park, C. L., Cohen, L. H., & Murch, R. L. (1996). Assessment and prediction of stress-related growth. *Journal of Personality, 64,* 71–105.

Peterson, G. R. (1997). Cognitive science: What one needs to know. *Zygon, 32,* 615–627.

Piedmont, R. L. (1999). Does spirituality represent the sixth factor of personality? Spiritual transcendence and the five-factor model. *Journal of Personality, 67,* 985–1014.

Pinker, S. (1997). *How the mind works.* New York: Norton.

Richards, N. (1992). *Humility.* Philadelphia: Temple University Press.

Sacks, H. L. (1979). The effects of spiritual exercises on the integration of the self-system. *Journal for the Scientific Study of Religion, 18,* 46–50.

Salovey, P., & Mayer, J. D. (1990). Emotional intelligence. *Imagination, Cognition, and Personality, 9,* 185–211.

Salovey, P., & Sluyter, D. J. (1997). *Emotional development and emotional intelligence.* New York: Basic Books.

Saver, J. L., & Rabin, J. (1997). The neural substrates of religious experience. *The Journal of Neuropsychiatry and Clinical Neurosciences, 9,* 498–510.

Scherwitz, L., & Canick, J. C. (1988). Self-reference and coronary heart disease risk. In B. K. Houston & C. R. Snyder (Eds.), *Type A behavior pattern: Research, theory, and intervention* (pp. 146–167). New York: Wiley.

Schimmel, S. (1997). *The seven deadly sins: Jewish, Christian, and classical reflections on human psychology.* New York: Oxford University Press.

Seligman, M. E. (1998, April). Positive social science. *APA Monitor, 29,* 2. 5.

Shulman, A. K. (1995). *Drinking the rain.* New York: Farrar. Straus & Giroux.

Slife, B., Hope, C., & Nebeker, S. (1997). *Examining the relationship between religious spirituality and psychological science.* Unpublished manuscript, Brigham Young University, Provo, UT.

Sternberg, R. J. (1990). *Metaphors of mind: Conceptions of the nature of intelligence.* New York: Cambridge University Press.

Sternberg, R. J. (1997). The concept of intelligence and its role in lifelong learning and success. *American Psychologist, 52,* 1030–1037.

Sternberg, R. J., & Ruzgis, P. (Eds.). (1994). *Personality and intelligence.* New York: Cambridge University Press.

Tellegen, A., Lykken, D. T., Bouchard, T. J., Jr., Wilcox, K., Segal, N., & Rich, S. (1988). Personality similarity in twins reared apart and together. *Journal of Personality and Social Psychology, 54,* 1031–1039.

Tillich, P. (1957). *Dynamics of faith.* New York: Harper & Row.

Tillich, P. (1963). *Christianity and the encounter of world religions.* New York: Columbia University Press.

Wallace, J. D. (1978). *Virtues and vices.* Ithaca, NY: Cornell University Press.

Waller, N. G., Kojetin, B. A., Bouchard, T. J., Jr., Lykken, D. T., & Tellegen, A. (1990). Genetic and environmental influences on religious interests, attitudes, and values: A study of twins reared apart and together. *Psychological Science, 1,* 1–5.

Walsh, R., & Vaughan, F. (1993). The art of transcendence: An introduction to common elements of transpersonal practices. *The Journal of Transpersonal Psychology, 25,* 1–9.

Walters, J. M., & Gardner, H. (1986). The theory of multiple intelligences: Some issues and answers. In R. J. Sternberg & R. K. Wagner (Eds.), *Practical intelligence* (pp. 163–182). New York: Cambridge University Press.

Weibust, P. S., & Thomas, L. E. (1996). Learning and spirituality in adulthood. In J. D. Sinnott (Ed.), *Interdisciplinary handbook of adult lifespan learning.* Westport, CT: Greenwood.

Weiss, H. M., & Knight, P. A. (1980). The utility of humility: Self-esteem, information search, and problem-solving efficiency. *Organizational Behavior and Human Decision Processes, 25,* 216–223.

Wilson, E. O. (1978). *On human nature.* Cambridge, MA: Harvard University Press.

Wong, P. T. P. (1998). Meaning-centered counseling. In P. T. P. Wong & P. S. Fry (Eds.), *The human quest for meaning* (pp. 395–435). Mahwah, NJ: Lawrence Erlbaum Associates, Inc.

Wulff, D. (1997). *Psychology of religion: Classic and contemporary* (2nd ed.). New York: Wiley.

Yang, S., & Sternberg, R. J. (1997). Conceptions of intelligence in ancient Chinese philosophy. *Journal of Theoretical and Philosophical Psychology, 17,* 101–119.

Zagzebski, L. T. (1996). *Virtues of the mind.* New York: Cambridge University Press.

THE INTERNATIONAL JOURNAL FOR THE PSYCHOLOGY OF RELIGION, *10*(1), 27–34

COMMENTARY

A Case Against Spiritual Intelligence

Howard Gardner

Graduate School of Education
Harvard University

Whether spirituality should be considered an intelligence depends upon definitions and criteria. Emmons tends to lump together different aspects of spirituality and also various facets of psychology. In my response, I demonstrate the advantages of teasing these concepts apart. Those aspects of spirituality that have to do with phenomenological experience or with desired values or behaviors are best deemed external to the intellectual sphere. A residue concerning the capacity to deal with existential issues may qualify as an intelligence. Emmons's overall enterprise is plausible and he raises many intriguing issues (e.g., sacredness, problem solving, the unifying potential of religion) that merit further investigation.

In the good old days, the concept of intelligence used to be unproblematic within academic psychology. The important niche occupied by intelligence was established by the success of the intelligence test, as first devised by Alfred Binet around the turn of the century, and then developed into an efficient, pragmatic instrument by psychometricians like Lewis Terman and David Wechsler (see Gardner, Kornhaber, & Wake, 1996, for a brief history). In light of this success, psychologists felt little need to create a theory of intelligence or to revise the tests of intelligence in a major way. Most were content to accept E. G. Boring's well-known assertion, in the heyday of scientific operationalism, that "intelligence is what the tests test." According to this consensus view, intelligence is a single capacity, often abbreviated as "g" for general intelligence; intelligence is largely inborn and there-

Requests for reprints should be sent to Howard Gardner, Larsen Hall, 2nd Floor, Harvard Graduate School of Education, Cambridge, MA 02138. E-mail: hgasst@pz.harvard.edu

fore difficult to alter; and psychologists can measure intelligence, from early in a subject's life through the administration of circumscribed instruments called IQ tests (cf. Herrnstein & Murray, 1994).

During the last 2 decades, the quiet consensus among psychologists has been rudely disrupted. New lines of investigation within neuroscience, cognitive science, anthropology, and psychology itself, combined with societal pressures, have challenged nearly every tenet about intelligence. Neuroscience has demonstrated the modular nature of the brain's (and presumably the mind's) organization; cognitive science has investigated the nature of expert knowledge in different domains; cross-cultural studies have revealed the quite different attitudes and analyses of intellect that have developed around the planet; psychologists have developed competing theories of intelligence; and social critiques of the possible biases built into psychometric instruments have all combined to put the "Intelligence Establishment" on the defensive, perhaps for the first time in a century.

Most revisions launched within psychology have attempted to play by the psychometrician's rules. That is, they have been based on tests—usually short-answer instruments—that tap the problem-solving capacities of subjects. Those who are critical of the standard view of intelligence favor a wide variety of questions or problems, and analyze the data in such a way as to call attention to the variety of intellectual factors: crystallized versus fluid intelligence (Horn, 1989); verbal versus mathematical versus spatial intelligence (Thurstone, 1938; Vernon, 1956); and contextual versus experiential versus computational intelligence (Sternberg, 1985), to cite three familiar examples.

My own work on multiple intelligences has proceeded in a different way (Gardner, 1993, 1999). Spurning tests and test scores, I have instead posed the question: How did the brain/mind evolve over many thousands of years, in order to allow individuals (and the species) to survive across a range of environments? Armed with this question, and drawing on data collected in the several sciences cited earlier, I initially identified seven forms of intelligence. In addition to the linguistic and logical–mathematical forms of intelligence that are at a premium in the schools, I proposed five additional intelligences (here listed along with specimen individuals who exemplify each intelligence): musical (composer, performer); spatial (sailor, architect); bodily-kinesthetic (athlete, dancer, surgeon); interpersonal (therapist, salesperson); and intrapersonal (individual with keen introspective skills). Recently, I have garnered evidence in favor of an eighth intelligence—that of the naturalist, the individual who readily recognizes patterns in the flora and fauna in the wild. I have considered evidence in favor of a ninth, or spiritual intelligence, only to conclude that this putative form of intelligence is problematic. In the process, however, I have become convinced that there may be an existential intelligence, that captures at least part of what individuals mean when they speak of spiritual concerns (see Gardner, 1999, for further discussion of these issues).

Clearly, in this endeavor, I am wrestling with many of the same issues as Emmons (this issue). Let me begin my commentary by affirming that Emmons's project is an eminently reasonable one and that he approaches it in a plausible way. Because I have reached a different conclusion, I will first recapitulate my own analysis, and then indicate where I agree with and where I differ from Emmons's enterprise.

I find it useful to distinguish among three connotations of the concept "spiritual." The first refers to the ability to realize certain physical states, such as those involved in meditation and other experiments with control of consciousness. Without doubt, such states exist and exhibit clear physiological concomitants. In my view, these states involve control over one's body and so are best thought of as expressions of bodily-kinesthetic intelligence.

The second aspect of spirituality has to do with the attainment of certain phenomenological states. The spiritual individual, on this account, feels "at one" with the universe, or loses himself in an oceanic state, or experiences a special link to God. Again, I have no doubt that such states are genuine, although I am uncertain about whether I have attained them myself. However, I do not want to include within the definition of an intelligence a certain "felt experience." Such feelings, I submit, are not intrinsic to the actual intelligence. Three individuals may evince exactly the same proficiency in the area of mathematics: The first describes feelings of unity with the cosmos; the second reports feelings of anxiety and pain, followed by a moment of release when a proof is achieved; the third reports no distinctive feelings whatsoever. On my analysis, all three are expressing their mathematical intelligence equivalently; they are differing in feeling states, which are best considered external to the intellectual realm.

"Core" to the intellectual realm is the capacity to carry out certain kinds of computations. Linguistic intelligence computes the sounds and sights of language; spatial intelligence computes positions and perspectives of entities in space; interpersonal intelligence computes the status, attitudes, and motivations of other individuals in relation to oneself; and so on. Each intelligence evolved because of the desirability of performing these computations efficiently. It seems to me that one aspect, or module, of mind may have evolved to perform computations (loosely speaking) on elements that transcend normal sensory perception, perhaps because they are too large or too small to be directly apprehended. I have labeled this form of intelligence "existential" because it seems yoked to the fact of our existence as individuals in the cosmos and our capacity to puzzle over that fact.

Somewhat to my surprise, "existential intelligence" qualifies well as an intelligence in light of the eight criteria that I have set forth in my writings (Gardner, 1993, chap. 4). Youngsters the world over raise fundamental questions about existence—Who are we?; Where do we come from?; What are we made of?; Why do we die?; and these questions are captured in symbolic systems such as myth, art, poetry, philosophy, and religion. Some individuals seem precocious in their capacity to pose such cosmic questions whereas others are mired in the mundane. There is little evidence for existential tendencies in nonhuman primates, but our own evolutionary antecedents, such as the Neanderthal, evinced signs of concern (if not "ultimate concern") in their burial rites.

My hesitation about proclaiming a ninth or existential intelligence derives chiefly from the lack of convincing evidence about brain structures and processes dedicated to this form of computation. As Emmons indicates, there are some hints about parts of the brain that may be important for investing significance in objects, and that may be linked to hyper- or hyporeligious behavior. However, in truth, such issues have not yet been much studied by neuroscientists, and so it is unclear whether these tendencies simply reflect a broader philosophical frame of mind, or whether they actually focus on capacities that can properly be limited to the existential or spiritual realm. For that reason, I have preferred to remain in a "holding pattern" and to speak, somewhat whimsically, of "8½ intelligences."

Having presented my own take on issues of spiritual or existential intelligence, let me now turn directly to Emmons's analysis. In several respects, I agree with and have gained from his own searching study of the spiritual domain. I particularly like his suggestion that the realm of the spiritual may provide a resource on which individuals may draw when they are trying to solve a problem. "Problem solving" is central to most concepts of intelligence, including mine, but the notion that spiritual considerations may facilitate problem solving is a novel and provocative one.

Here, the psychologist in me calls for an "unpacking" of a pregnant suggestion. Are there ways in which one can show that spiritual resources are being drawn on? How are they being drawn on? Do they necessarily lead to better or swifter problem solutions, or might they be misleading? Which sources or resources can substitute for spiritual ones? In short, can one offer a computational (or procedural) account of the invoking of spiritual resources in the formulation or solving of a problem?

I am also sympathetic to Emmons's proposal that the various facets of spirituality may cluster together. Such coalescence seems to me to be a characteristic of intelligences, more broadly; they each consist of various separable core operations which, given the nature of human experience, tend to accrue and to become organized into a totality. Thus, musical intelligence entails sensitivity to harmony, rhythm, timbre, overall composition; interpersonal intelligence comprises understanding of motivation, ability to work cooperatively, interpretation of others' goals. In each case, individuals might initially excel in just one of these core components; but sustained functioning in the world tends to facilitate these core components working together. I endorse Emmons's suggestion that the realm (or domain) of religion is constructed precisely so as to encourage a concatenation of the several facets of spirituality.

Attention to the sacred, and the capacity to demarcate certain aspects of life as sacred, seems to me to call attention to an important and neglected aspect of human psychology. Again, I am stimulated to raise further questions. How do we know what is sacred? Do parents and transitional objects qualify in early life? Friends and hobbies and favored vacation spots later on? Are there independent grounds for delineating what is sacred and separating it from the profane? To what extent can the characteristics of the sacred be discerned across historical periods or cultural divides?

Having indicated those portions of Emmons's analysis that I find instructive, I should now mention those that appear to me to be problematic. From my vantage point, it is very important to keep separate the *power* of computational capacities, from the *uses* to which they are put. Both Goethe and Goebbels displayed excellent intelligence in the German language: Goethe used his linguistic gifts to write estimable poetry and drama whereas Goebbels used his talent to foment hatred. Both Mao Zedong and Mahatma Gandhi were gifted in the interpersonal domain, and yet, again, they made quite divergent uses of these talents. In his otherwise admirable book *Emotional Intelligence*, Daniel Goleman (1995) lays out the five features of this form of intelligence but then, from my vantage point, muddies the water by failing to distinguish adequately between high levels of analysis and performance, on the one hand, and the proclivity to lead an admirable life on the other.

Emmons also blurs the line between the descriptive and the prescriptive. For the most part, he focuses on abilities that all of us have to some degree, and that certain individuals possess to a pronounced extent. But at other times, he focuses on capacities that he clearly believes are admirable (e.g., humility). I endorse analyses that make a sharp distinction between these two realms. Whether we like it or not, among the individuals who seem to have had strong spiritual intelligence (in Emmons's sense) are ones who are frankly antisocial, psychopathic, or to use an old-fashioned word, evil. In his book *Feet of Clay*, Anthony Storr (1996) illustrates the difficulty of distinguishing between those who use their spiritual intelligence in a creative, as opposed to destructive, manner.

Emmons builds part of his argument on behavioral genetics—a line of analysis that should be invoked only with utmost caution in the human realm. There is no question that the techniques of behavioral genetics are valuable when brought to bear on data that have been obtained under strictly controlled conditions—for example, in studies of plant or animal breeding. Such studies are, however, quite properly forbidden with human beings. Even the most reliable studies with humans—those comparing identical twins with fraternal twins, or identical twins reared together with identical twins reared apart—do not satisfy the requirements for controlled experiments. Consider, for example, that all identical twins share the same womb environment for approximately 9 months, and that even identical twins reared apart are not randomly assigned to environments. Consider, as well, that twins are aware of their twinship and have the prerogative of either exploiting or rebelling against this status. None of these conditions can be adequately controlled. And so the fact that religiosity seems to some extent to be a heritable trait cannot serve as a basis for conclusions about the brain or genetic basis of spirituality. There are simply too many steps between the data and the conclusions.

Emmons suggests that humility may be an adaptive characteristic. I value humility greatly, and wish that I and those around me would display more of it. However, I am not convinced that humility is in general an adaptive trait. Indeed, as I observe life around us in the United States today, it seems far easier to mount a case in favor of the proposition that pride or hubris is adaptive. At any rate, it is difficult to envision tests that could allow us to draw confident conclusions about the relevant value of humility versus hubris in different contexts at different historical times—let alone to try to reason backwards to the social situation that obtained in small bands of *Homo erectus* or *Homo habilis* living in East Africa millions of years ago.

I think that it would be useful to observe a distinction that I have come to make between an intelligence and a domain. An intelligence is a biological potential to analyze certain kinds of information in certain kinds of ways. Intelligences are activated, or not, depending on the culture in which one lives and one's own value system. Domains (or disciplines or crafts) are organized activities in a culture wherein one can rank individuals in terms of their relative expertise. Academic disciplines, arts, crafts, and hobbies are all examples of domains.

Applied to the present topic, spiritual intelligence would entail a potential to pay attention to content that is deemed sacred and to do so in certain ways (e.g., through transcendent fusion with sacred materials). The society supplies various domains, including organized religion or meditative practices, within which the individual can choose to utilize the spiritual intelligence. On rare occasions, an individual might create his or her own domain.

On this analysis, one can then consider the various domains available in the culture (ranging from Judaism to Shamanism to yoga) and probe the extent to which various intelligences are (or are not) brought to bear as an individual enters and then masters a given domain. Alerted to this distinction, one is less likely to confound what is essentially a mode of processing with a man- (or God-) created activity. Religion becomes not the defining characteristic of spiritual intelligence, but rather one of a number of domains in which that form of intelligence can be utilized.

Strong feelings exist on the general topic of whether there is, or is not, a spiritual intelligence—and, if so, how best to delineate it—and it is not likely that these will be easily altered. Some of these strong feelings probably reflect deep belief systems. I would suggest, however, that the differences might also reflect personal stylistic preferences.

Put succinctly, I am intellectually a splitter, whereas I suspect Emmons is a lumper. That is, I like to make distinctions and I also believe that intellectual progress is likely to follow if the *right* distinctions are proposed. My assumption is that

Emmons is attracted to the discovery of relations among items, perhaps especially far-stretching relations, and that he believes intellectual progress is tied to these connections.

Let me offer two "cases in point." In reading through his article, I was struck by the large number of allusions to items that fall under the rubric of spirituality. Emmons (this issue) speaks of "virtuous behavior," "ultimate concern," "intimacy with the divine," "personal striving," "the long view," "humility," and "integration of self concept"—and these are but a partial sampling. I may have pleasant associations to many of these phrases but I am far from certain that they all refer to the same concept and, indeed, I would appreciate having them teased apart.

A second case in point has to do with the sweep of the term *intelligence* itself. I plead guilty to the charge of having stretched the term myself. Still, I believe that it belongs most properly in the realm of cognition, which is currently connected to forms of information processing. Emmons, however, is much more promiscuous in his use of the term *intelligence*. As I read his opening pages, I note that he sees intelligence as tied to motivation, emotions, personality, and morality. Now I have no doubt that if these terms make scientific sense, it is important to be able to connect them to one another. But that is a different endeavor from one that seeks to erase the distinctions among these psychological dimensions. I am leery of so stretching the term *intelligence* that it sacrifices its primary ties with cognition and instead becomes cognate with the human psyche in all of its wondrous dimensions.

Finally, I have to record my own hesitation about the closing of Emmons's article. I sympathize with his interest in promoting the scholarly study of religion and I believe that his own article contributes to that worthy end. However, the desire to stimulate a line of study does not permit one to conflate analysis with advocacy. Spirituality is worthy of study as an intelligence if that lens illuminates its nature; the possibility that it may encourage more study of religion, or improve religion's place in the world, is not in my mind a proper rationale. I know whereof I speak because my own work on multiple intelligences has often been drawn on as a justification for arts education. I happen to be a staunch advocate of arts education, but I have often had to explain that there is no such thing as artistic intelligence.

In sum, then, I applaud Emmons's investigation although, in the end, I come to a different set of conclusions. We read the data somewhat differently, and my criteria for an intelligence are less flexible than his. I also believe that our different conclusions follow, to some extent, from different intellectual styles, with myself as an inveterate splitter and Emmons, I suspect, as an avid lumper. A number of the points that he makes seem well worth following up through further analytic and empirical investigations; I hope that he is invigorated to pursue these consequential issues by the exchanges in these pages.

REFERENCES

Gardner, H. (1993). *Frames of mind: The theory of multiple intelligences*. New York: Basic Books.

Gardner, H. (1999). *Intelligence reframed: Multiple intelligences for the new millenium*. New York: Basic Books.

Gardner, H., Kornhaber, M., & Wake, W. (1996). *Intelligence: Multiple perspectives*. San Antonio, TX: Harcourt Brace.

Goleman, D. (1995). *Emotional intelligence*. New York: Bantam.

Herrnstein, R., & Murray, C. (1994). *The bell curve*. New York: Free Press.

Horn, J. (1989). Models of intelligence. In R. Linn (Ed.), *Intelligence: Measurement, theory, and public policy*. Urbana: University of Illinois Press.

Sternberg, R. (1985). *Beyond IQ*. New York: Cambridge University Press.

Storr, A. (1996). *Feet of clay*. New York: Free Press.

Thurstone, L. L. (1938). *Primary mental abilities*. Chicago: University of Chicago Press.

Vernon, P. E. (1956). *The measurement of abilities*. London: University of London Press.

THE INTERNATIONAL JOURNAL FOR THE PSYCHOLOGY OF RELIGION, *10*(1), 35–46

COMMENTARY

Spiritual Intelligence as a Theory of Individual Religion: A Case Application

Susan Kwilecki

Department of Philosophy and Religious Studies
Radford University

This article considers the utility of Emmons's theory of "spiritual intelligence" for the analysis of the religions of individuals. The hypothesis is divided into a proposed *description*, *explanation*, and *assessment of the consequences* of personal faith. The spiritual biography of Gladys Day, a contemporary African American Pentecostal, provides an empirical format for the consideration of each formulation. Accordingly, the "core components" receive high marks for capturing the essential dynamics of spiritual growth. However, the explanation of personal religion as an expression of a universal capacity for transcendence is relatively weak vis-à-vis one that identifies immediate biographical causes. Attentiveness to differences in religious and secular conceptions of health and adaptation would improve Emmons's assessment of the fruits of spiritual intelligence.

My field is not psychology but religious studies, a multidisciplinary investigation of the area of human concern Emmons (this issue) describes as spirituality[1]—devotion to transcendent forces credited with ultimacy. Accordingly, I will comment on the usefulness of Emmons's conceptualization of spirituality as an intel-

Requests for reprints should be sent to Susan Kwilecki, Department of Philosophy and Religious Studies, Radford University, Radford, VA 24142. E-mail: skwileck@runet.edu

[1]To designate the human concern with ultimate, divine, or transcendent realities, I use *religion* and *religiousness* interchangeably with *spirituality*. For present purposes, whether or not an individual is affiliated with a religious institution—a common criterion for distinguishing *religion* from *spirituality*—is insignificant.

ligence for describing and explaining the religions of individuals, the focus of my own research.

As an abstraction, spiritual intelligence is intended to represent a huge and amorphous class of phenomena. Images come to mind of Jehovah's Witnesses knocking on doors to announce the apocalypse, Jain monks starving themselves to death, Mother Teresa succoring the dying, New Agers recalling past lives, Islamic terrorists plotting vengeance on the United States, yogis immobilized in blissful trance—and, of course, average Americans reciting blessings over meals and filing into pews on Sunday morning.

How can we reasonably assess the adequacy of any theoretical construct to such a range of data? My proposal is modest—the application of the concept of spiritual intelligence to a single religious life. The case will serve as an empirical medium for bringing to light what I perceive as general strengths and weaknesses of the hypothesis. For this reason, I have selected not a typical believer, but one whose spirituality is sufficiently developed to provide an unequivocal, substantial case of what the theory purports to cover.

GLADYS DAY (1925–)[2]

Gladys Day was born into the Black lower class in rural Georgia, a life station of restricted opportunities for material security and personal development. However, not poverty but illness and interpersonal antagonism led her to seek religious consolation.

Throughout her life, according to Gladys, her family and peers have continually rejected and betrayed her. Before her spiritual baptism, she sometimes responded violently. Chronic emotional instability, punctuated by symptoms of dissociation and conversion illness, has caused many, including her husband and members of her church, to consider her "crazy." Hers is a test case of the power of spiritual intelligence to solve problems. Let me summarize the phases of her religious growth, editing for saliency to Emmons's construct.

From Gladys's recollections, she seems to have been an isolated and obstreperous child. "I never played much, you know, like a lot of other children. I just sit and look. But I was mean about fighting," she said. Her mother, she recounted, unjustly favored her two sisters, who would gang up and "try to whup" her, whereupon she would "take they heads and just butt 'em together." In her teens, she gave birth out of wedlock to two babies by different fathers.

---

[2]To protect the anonymity of participants, I have changed the names of people and churches. I met Gladys Day in 1987, when I was living in her hometown. Over the following decade, I conducted four lengthy interviews and communicated informally by mail and telephone. I attended services at her church and interviewed her eldest daughter and the daughter's husband. For more detailed portrayals of Gladys's faith see Kwilecki (1994) and Kwilecki (1999, pp. 207–220).

Adolescence brought the first of an unending series of dreams, voices, and visions heralding an impending death. Initially the messages frightened her, Gladys said, for she did not understand what she now knows, that they come from God. During this period, another lifelong religious habit began, seeking and claiming to have achieved supernatural vengeance against enemies. When her father insulted her, young Gladys asked God to "trouble" his food so that he could not eat. According to Gladys, God complied. Amazed and intimidated, her father apologized.

In 1948, Gladys married Ozell Day, employed at the time in a peanut mill. Over the next 7 years, she gave birth annually, a series of pregnancies that damaged her health. In addition to uterine hemorrhaging, she suffered episodes of temporary blindness and immobility that baffled doctors. She was unable to run her house and care for her children. "Everybody thought I was crazy!" Gladys recalled. She was well enough, however, to wage war over Ozell's infidelities. "When I got a little mad with him, I would set him up. He'd have to run. Or try to shoot him. I cut his hands up so bad one time," she confessed, "he couldn't work. Trying to cut his throat." Her children considered her "the meanest woman in the world." In retrospect, Gladys realized that, despite participation in a neighborhood Methodist church, "I didn't have no keeper then.... I didn't have no power over no kind of spirits. I didn't have no power over nothing."

Her journey towards spiritual empowerment began in 1957, when she sought healing of the aforementioned symptoms under the tent of Bishop Theodore Wells, charismatic founder of Signs and Wonders Tabernacle, a regional Black Pentecostal sect. When Wells touched her, Gladys said, "look like something just went all through me and just went on out." By the next morning, the debilitating sickness had disappeared. For Gladys, the sudden cure attested that "the Lord was really real," and validated the Bishop's supernatural authority and teachings. The Bishop and his wife befriended Gladys, and by the end of the crusade, she was determined to pursue the Pentecostal goal of holiness, a personal state of moral purity and blessedness facilitated by the indwelling of the Holy Spirit.

The Bishop returned to his headquarters in Macon, about 2 hr away. Over the next 15 years, Gladys contacted him occasionally by telephone and mail. In the meantime, after futilely seeking guidance towards holiness within local congregations, she began to hear the voices of "peoples of the Old Testament, the prophets," who, after she read the Bible, "would come and tell ... the meaning of [a] lot of stuff."

In 1972, her grandson's murder brought Gladys's spiritual quest to a climax. Weeks before the death, voices and dreams warned her of imminent disaster. One morning, Gladys was babysitting the child; his mother, returning to pick him up, found him strangled to death on Gladys's doorstep. "We don't know what happened," Gladys told me. The police, however, theorized that someone in the family had killed him to collect life insurance. As a suspect, Gladys endured months of interrogation and surveillance. Under the strain, she prayed desperately for divine help. Soon the Bishop (acting, according to Gladys, on instructions God sent to his wife in a dream) returned to her hometown. At a tent service, Gladys spoke in tongues, signifying the baptism of the Holy Spirit, and became a founding member of a local Signs and Wonders congregation.

Shortly after her spiritual baptism, a dream and the chattering of voices after she read the Bible ("Inside it would just go on and on.... I couldn't stop it from talking") convinced Gladys she had been called to preach. She assumed the religious role, modeled on the careers of the Hebrew prophets and Pentecostal teachings, of God's agent, anointed to proclaim his will to the unregenerate—a pivotal step in spiritual development.

The new "anointed" identity transposed the raw materials of habitual social confrontation and isolation into cosmic drama. As the voice of righteousness in a wicked world, Gladys expected and accepted treachery and rejection from others, now recast as sinners. "Them that live godly must suffer persecution," she explained; indeed, she paraphrased scripture, "Your enemies is your household." The redeeming feature of the prophetic self-image was the guarantee that if she obeyed God, he would protect her from adversaries. "If you do something to me now—and I don't care who you is," she declared, "if I can hold my peace and not talk back, God gon' work on you. Just as sure as I'm sitting on this seat!"

Gladys related numerous episodes in which she boldly castigated sinners, was duly scorned, but eventually triumphed. Usually victory was realized as Gladys gleaned information and heeded advice from inner voices (now identified with the Holy Spirit); a favorable turn of events indicated the hand of God. Nonbelievers would recognize the Spirit's directions as common sense, intuition, or the intrusion of unconscious wishes, and reported miracles as coincidences. Let me summarize two ordeals that stimulated both the capacity for virtue Emmons describes and conversion symptoms.

In 1986, Gladys received the revelation that her middle-aged and married pastor was having an affair with her young daughter, Janelle. "God gon' strike you down!" she confronted Elder Daniels, who denied the charge and castigated Gladys from the pulpit. Janelle, likewise, maintained her innocence. No one believed Gladys until the couple left town together. Then, instead of crediting her insight, family and church members accused her of facilitating the affair, "cloakin" for the lovers. "You see me, honey? I been pierced!" she recalled her devastation. Had she been unsaved, she speculated, "I'da killed [Elder Daniels]."

However, she herself nearly died. "I had a death spirit talk to me and told me I was gonna die over that," she related. Once before, Gladys had fallen victim to a "death spirit," and been cured by the Bishop's prayer. This time, the spirit ordered her to gaze in the mirror, where her image appeared corpselike, with shrunken skin and blue circles under her eyes. She could not swallow food and was unable to get out of bed unassisted. When the Bishop prayed for her over the telephone, her symptoms disappeared.

However, the ordeal was not over. In time, Janelle and Elder Daniels married. As a Christian, Gladys knew she had to make peace with her new son-in-law. "But," she wondered, "how was I gon' do that with a hurt heart?" Visiting the couple for the first time, she prayed, "Lord, I got to forgive. And I've got to let him know it to his face." Virtue triumphed: "I greeted [Elder Daniels] and told him I loved him." Gladys summarized the moral of the story: "God gon' heal that wound. But, see, you got to have power over that getting tore up all the time. Getting angry—see?"

A second bout of illness and moral struggle began in 1993, when Ozell took a new mistress, Louise, a neighbor Gladys had considered her friend. Once again, the Holy Spirit alerted Gladys of the affair. Following the Spirit's order to interrupt a rendezvous, she marched Ozell home, warning, "God just ain't gon' let you do me any kind of way ... and he not show me what's going on!" Soon she discovered black "dust" scattered in her food, bed, and personal belongings, which, she said, caused her to feel drunk; smell a disgusting odor; and lose her hair, appetite, and sometimes sight. A vision revealed that Louise was performing "voodoo" against her.

Instead of sympathizing, according to Gladys, family and church members "talk[ed] as if my mind was gone." Had she been unsaved, she reflected, "I woulda killed my husband and I woulda killed that lady." However, the Spirit chastened, "Don't use your hands for nothing but to praise me!" She considered hexing Ozell's food, but was warned, "Don't do it!" She obeyed.

Prayer from the Bishop and a victorious visionary confrontation with Louise's spirit brought temporary relief. Then she learned that God planned to end the situation once and for all: "The Lord told me he was gon' get rid of [Louise]." On the Spirit's order to prepare Louise for death, Gladys attempted to evangelize her; Louise responded by seeking a peace warrant against her. A few weeks later, Louise died from a heart attack. Seeing Ozell's grief, Gladys felt sad. Instantly, the Spirit corrected her: "Hush it! That is my doing. It is marvelous in my sight."

IS GLADYS SPIRITUALLY INTELLIGENT?

How well does Emmons's conceptualization of spiritual intelligence describe and explain Gladys's religious history? To answer, I distill the theory into three assertions: (a) humans pursue transcendence through several specific abilities or core components; (b) these abilities are innate in humans, the product of species-wide physiological and evolutionary forces; and (c) often, but not always, these abilities facilitate effective problem solving, adaptation, and health. As a theory, spiritual intelligence contains a *description*, an *explanation*, and an *assessment of the consequences* of individual religion, each of which I consider with respect to Gladys's case.

Description

Emmons provisionally names five core components of spiritual intelligence (see Emmons, this issue, Table 1, p. 10). Gladys exhibits all five. Indeed, together they precisely and comprehensively describe the dynamics through which her faith evolved.

A capacity for religious experiences was the *sine qua non* of Gladys's faith. Premonitory voices, dreams, and visions introduced her to a mysterious clairvoyant force. A curative emotional response to the laying-on of hands stimulated her pursuit of holiness. Glossolalia signified success. Dreams and voices launched and sustained her prophetic endeavors.

In short, Gladys experienced a continuous stream of peculiar auditory and visual impressions she construed as supernatural in origin. Thus she enjoyed constant sensory access to transcendent realities many believers grasp only in abstract; on-the-spot vocalizations relieved the characteristic uncertainty of spiritual striving with precise situational orders. Emmons's "ability to experience heightened states of consciousness" captures the critical experiential basis of Gladys's spirituality, albeit in language that seems pallid vis-à-vis her style of divine encounter.

Another core component frames an equally vital force in her religious career, the "ability to utilize spiritual resources to solve problems." The successful faith healing in 1957 was pivotal; the ensuing quest for holiness was essentially pragmatic, a bid for blessings and power. Over the years, she utilized a range of Pentecostal coping resources: faith healing; the promise of miracles; interpretations of suffering as a badge of, or means to, godliness; the expectation of guidance and fortitude from the indwelling Holy Spirit; and, not least of all, the assurance of divine protection contingent on obedience. Only partially reported here, her spiritual problem solving runs the gamut from shouting "Jesus" to ward off an attacking dog, to identifying with Job, whose troubles brought him closer to God. Whereas the experiential component specifies a central mechanism of Gladys's spiritual growth, this one captures its master motivation.

The other core elements—the abilities to "transcend the physical and material," "sanctify everyday experience," and "be virtuous"—specify cumulative effects of Gladys's constant religious experiences and coping. Together they describe what I consider the most spectacular development in Gladys's religious biography: the transformation of the vindictiveness of a tortured soul into celestial gallantry. The capacities to "transcend the physical and material" and "sanctify everyday experience" enabled Gladys to understand (for her) routine backbiting and marital discord and infidelity on a grand scale, as symptoms of humanity's estrangement from its Creator. The prophetic obligation to uphold righteousness tempered previously overwhelming retaliatory impulses. Spiritually restrained, she demonstrated the "capacity to be virtuous" when she forgave Elder Daniels and waited for God to handle Louise.

In my view, the core components of spiritual intelligence constitute a powerful descriptive tool for the study of personal religion. Singly and together, they identify elements common and salient to the growth and expression of piety across lives. The utility of the core components reflects, I think, Emmons's attentiveness to the self-proclaimed, deliberate intentions of believers, for which he is to be congratulated.

There are other strategies for conceptualizing the faculty that enables transcendence. For example, James Fowler (1981) traced the development over the life span of "faith," the human capacity to seek and impose meaning, which overlaps with spiritual intelligence. However, Fowler focused on the syntax rather than the content of meaning systems. Different forms of faith are identified in terms of cognitive structures of which the believer is unconscious, not professed convictions. Thus, an individual's faith is assessed by standards foreign to him or her (e.g., logical style), to the neglect of conscious centers of value and striving. In my experience the latter, not the former, hold the key to understanding the evolution of personal world views (see Kwilecki, 1988; 1999, pp. 20–21, 263–264).

The close correspondence between the core components and believers' experiences and intentions, in my opinion, elevates spiritual intelligence head and shoulders above rival concepts of a pan-human capacity to apprehend ultimate truths and values, such as Fowler's. I cannot think of deletions or additions I would make to Emmons's list of five core components.

Explanation

Why did Gladys Day become religious? That is, what empirical conditions and factors propelled her towards the transcendent view of life described earlier? The theory of spiritual intelligence answers, in essence, *her humanity*. Personal spirituality is an expression of a generic human potential for transcendence. Emmons joins a large and distinguished group of theorists who account for the ubiquity of religion across cultures and time with a universal brushstroke (see Kwilecki, 1999, pp. 31–32).

My own attempts to explain personal religion have led me elsewhere. Putative universals seldom provide the best available explanation of an actual human event. If we ask, for example, why Lincoln was assassinated, an answer in terms of Freud's aggressive instinct is not nearly as precise or compelling as one that delineates Booth's motives and actions. The process of spiritual development is no different. Despite the aforementioned similarities across lives, factual intricacies and variations demand discriminate explanation.

Examining life after life, I have found that specific biographical configurations provide the most direct and exact explanations of an individual's spirituality. To the extent that these can be abstractly summarized, they generally consist of interactions between personal factors, such as a particular temperament or need, and collective religious teachings that meet the need or externalize the disposition (Kwilecki, 1999).

Space does not permit full elaboration of the explanation I offer for Gladys's religion (see Kwilecki, 1999, pp. 208–211, 219–220). Let me briefly consider but one element of her faith—a critical core component, the capacity for "heightened states of consciousness." What were the psychic roots of Gladys's marked susceptibility to divine encounter? Emmons proposes a generic human capacity for transcendent states. However, the biographical data suggest a more obvious source of many (but not all) of Gladys's religious experiences—chronic ego fragmentation.

A number of the voices Gladys credited to supernatural sources appear to be unassimilated parts of her own psyche, for example, the instructions of the prophets after she read the Bible, the death spirit's prediction of her demise, the Holy Spirit's revelations of Janelle's and Ozell's affairs, his decree of Louise's death and mandate of self-restraint. Collective religious teachings (folk, biblical, and Pentecostal) to which she was exposed provided labels and explanations for the (to her) alien communications and dictated appropriate response. Thus, in my view, many of Gladys's "heightened states of consciousness" evolved as she drew upon religious, notably Pentecostal, attributions to self-explain subjective raw materials produced by dissociation.

Unlike Emmons's generic capacity for transcendent states, this account reflects the specific characteristics of the experiences in question, and links them to other aspects of Gladys's religious career that likewise seem to pivot on poor ego integration, such as the crucial faith healing in 1957. This is not to say that, at some level, somehow, a generic human potential for transcendent states was not operative in the experiences under consideration. However, the particularistic account makes this hypothesis unnecessary.

In sum, if each individual's spiritual development may be explained in terms of specific biographical dynamics—and I believe it can—then, unless one prefers the esoteric to the concrete, there is no reason to posit a generic spiritual capacity. This explanatory weakness is, of course, not peculiar to Emmons's formulation but inherent in deductive theorizing (for my alternative, see Kwilecki, 1999, pp. 24–26, 35–38).

Assessment of the Consequences of Spirituality

Intelligence, as commonly conceived, implies an adaptive or problem-solving capacity. Hence, although he recognizes "the possible harmfulness of religious beliefs or spiritually oriented lifestyles," Emmons (this issue) stresses their salutary effects. "Spiritual intelligence has been conceived of in this article as largely a positive construct" (p. 19). Here he joins company with a growing number of contemporary researchers impressed by the prophylactic and remedial power of religion against all manner of human ills (in addition to Emmons's citations, see Benson, 1996; Dossey, 1993; Koenig, 1997; Matthews, 1998).

As a student of religious traditions and lives, this strikes me as a misguided effort to sanitize religion, an oversimplification of an inherently paradoxical reality. There is no denying that spirituality can be of immeasurable valuable in sustaining optimism, dignity, and morality in the face of obstacles and tragedy. I have seen it bestow on individuals who had every reason to despair a "new zest which adds itself like a gift to life" (James, 1958, p. 401).

Of course, everyone agrees, religion sometimes has deleterious effects. However, in my view, the ambiguity of the situation exceeds the commonplace that religion hurts some and helps others. Even when it palliates and invigorates—indeed, precisely when it does this best—I am claiming, spirituality simultaneously compromises mental health and effective problem solving. The negative consequences to which I am referring are not accidental, but inexorably contained in the distinctive way religion delivers its benefits, namely by redirecting the ambitions and hopes of the sufferer to a realm beyond the senses and reason.

Insofar as spirituality is strong enough to fortify, it exacts a price in what is arguably our most adaptive faculty—rationality, the capacity to reach conclusions about the world by reasoning critically on evidence. Alcock (1992) summarizes the paradox of spiritual adaptation or coping: "While religious faith helps many to face their daily struggles … and to accept their misfortunes, it would appear to the nonbeliever that the believer relies on fantasy … to confront problems and allay fears" (p. 124). This, of course, was Freud's objection which, like the contemporary endorsement of religion, was unbalanced, but based on accurate observation.

Gladys's case illustrates the inherent liabilities of spiritually derived strengths. In many respects, becoming spiritual made Gladys happier, stronger, and healthier. Conceiving of herself as God's agent enhanced her sense of personal power, bestowed order on a chaotic inner life, and facilitated the control of violent impulses. Was she disappointed or content with her life? I once queried. "Well, now it is [good]," she replied. "Sometime I have a little trouble, though, but it don't last." Asked to characterize herself as either an optimist or a pessimist, she chose the former: "I be expecting good things. Course, now, bad things come up. But I be expecting good things."

Nevertheless, were she a client, few mental health professionals would recommend discharge. However comforting her faith may be, it is unrealistic. God has not delivered her from a bad marriage and continual strife with her peers. Indeed, the rejuvenating self-image of holy warrior virtually guarantees future confrontations; someone within her purview is bound to be violating commandments. Further, it blinds her to immediate (and perhaps remediable) causes of her social maladjustment—a personal volatility and eccentricity rooted in mental illness. Despite the positive effects of identifying her inner voices with the Holy Spirit, she remains the imperceptive servant of impulse, now unexamined biblical mandates. In this case, the "ability to sanctify everyday experience" blocks the realistic self-awareness that mental health professionals typically try to instill.

Whether psychotherapy could help Gladys is unknown. However, this much is clear: Religion has at best recast her problems into a form immediately less painful and harmful; it has not relieved their causes. All things considered, the effects of spirituality on Gladys's health are paradoxical. The devotion that strengthens and restrains simultaneously impedes realistic and possibly more effective coping.

Beyond the problem of disconfirming evidence, which he acknowledges, the chief weakness in Emmons's assessment of the consequences of spirituality, in my view, is a failure to recognize the distinctive nature of spirituality as a mode of adaptation. He seems to assume that psychologists and believers agree on what constitutes adaptive behavior, that the objectives of therapy and spirituality coincide. This is not so.

Religions promise the world and more to those who properly connect with elusive, mysterious, intangible powers. Healthiness and effective problem solving, indeed the very problems humans have to solve, are construed in terms of this supernatural, or transcendent, dimension, and the means to them are equally quixotic.

For example, the Bible portrays the central human dilemma as constantly having to choose between obeying God and egocentric satisfactions. The healthy, well-adjusted person is one who, like Abraham and Jesus, obeys even commandments that from a human standpoint seem outrageous and destructive. The maladaptive consequences of autonomous decision making are clear from the stories of Adam and Eve, Saul, and Jonah, not to mention the collective disasters of ancient Israel.

The exhortation, across traditions, to imitate the extreme devotion of saviors and founders—for example, Jesus's or Husaine's martyrdom, Abraham's willingness to sacrifice Isaac, the Buddha's abandonment of his family and political duties, Muhammad's forcible subjugation of unbelieving Meccans—underscores the divergence of spiritual and secular concepts of the good life. Even when religious objectives include self-evident advantages like physical health, social integration, and material prosperity, commonly prescribed means to these ends have often been impractical, if not harmful, for example, animal and human sacrifice, painful initiation ordeals, holy wars, the execution of heretics and witches, following the advice of mediums obtained in aberrant mental states, and slavish obedience to persons and laws. These widespread collective practices, let me stress, are not regrettable accidents in religious life, but requirements for spiritual adaptation and health historically conceived.

Orientation to a transcendent realm makes spiritual striving intrinsically different from, and sometimes inimical to, mainstream psychological ideals of mental health and adaptation. The latter derive from a secular or naturalistic view of humans and the problems they must solve. The healthy individual is, essentially, one who has maximized his or her natural potentials for realism, love, idealism, inner integration and balance—in harmony with physical, social, and psychic constraints (Batson, Schoenrade, & Ventis, 1993, pp. 235–239; Jahoda, 1958, pp. 22–64). Psychological healthiness and adaptation can be empirically assessed in terms of, say, marital or job satisfaction, unlike nirvana or Christian salvation, which have supernatural dimensions inaccessible to human scrutiny. Adaptation does not require the avoidance of demons or appeasement of ancestral spirits, because these beings are not self-evident structures of the environment. Ginsburg's (as cited in Jahoda, 1958) definition of environmental mastery—"the ability to hold a job, have a family, keep out of trouble with the law, and enjoy the usual opportunities for pleasure" (p. 55)—would outrage believers from many traditions.

Thus, in my view, the issue Emmons addresses in the section entitled "Is There an Optimal Level of Spiritual Intelligence?" runs much deeper than the dilemma of what to do with intolerant fundamentalists or cult suicides. Again, the problem lies in a confusion of religious with secular understandings of well-being, so that spiritual striving is expected to produce outcomes that meet psychological criteria of health and adaptation. Although this does indeed happen, there is nothing intrinsic to spirituality that guarantees it; indeed, as I have suggested, much in the history of traditions belies this expectation.

Emmons's stopgap proposal that harmful spirituality is the result of imbalance, excess, or character flaws, reflects the same troubling conflation of religious and psychological criteria of health. He misconstrues as excess what may be required by a tradition for spiritual achievement, for example, the intolerant denouncement of sin, or obedience unto death. Thus, he implicitly endorses healthy moderation over the full-blown devotion of prophets, saints, and saviors who set the standards believers are to follow.

Given a discriminate definition of adaptiveness or effective problem solving, Emmons's claim that spiritual intelligence is adaptive would be more tenable. By discriminate definition, I mean one that recognizes and somehow accommodates the difference in spiritual and secular modes of conceiving and actualizing human potential. On the one hand, he must take seriously the believer's orientation to a supernatural environment—which makes every spiritual act, no matter how apparently bizarre or destructive, ultimately adaptive. On the other hand, if spiritual intelligence is to function as a psychological concept, he must honor scientific empiricism, which means measuring adaptiveness in terms of consequences in this world. Arriving at such a definition will be tricky, but not impossible. In all, the adaptive component of spiritual intelligence must be qualified, I think, but not surrendered.

Let me conclude by returning to the confession with which I began: I am not a psychologist. The prospect, undoubtedly appealing to many readers, of integrating and expanding branches of psychology by conceiving of spirituality as an intelligence does not move me. I have no loyalty to any particular academic discipline or method. As a scholar, I am concerned only with doing justice to the data of religious life. From my immersion in that data, through training in the scriptures and histories of traditions and fieldwork with fervent believers, I have developed a perception of religion as high drama. Devoting scarce resources to powers and destinations one cannot sensibly or rationally apprehend strikes me as at once the most heroic and foolish thing a person can do. The causes and consequences of this radical approach to life will always remain partially obscure. Insofar as they can be observed, the origins of spirituality are infinitely varied and complex, and its effects typically paradoxical.

As universalistic theories of religion go, spiritual intelligence has much to recommend it, and it can be improved. However, I remain skeptical of the bare feasibility and wisdom of attempting to capture religion through any single theoretical construct, be it cognitive structures, object relations, or, in this case, intelligence.

REFERENCES

Alcock, J. E. (1992). Religion and rationality. In J. F. Schumaker (Ed.), *Religion and mental health* (pp. 122–131). New York: Oxford University Press.

Batson, C. C., Schoenrade, P., & Ventis, W. L. (1993). *Religion and the individual: A social–psychological perspective.* New York: Oxford University Press.

Benson, H., with Stark, M. (1996). *Timeless healing: The power and biology of belief.* New York: Fireside.

Dossey, L. (1993). *Healing words: The power of prayer and the practice of medicine.* New York: Harper Paperbacks.

Fowler, J. (1981). *Stages of faith.* New York: Harper & Row.

Jahoda, M. (1958). *Current concepts of positive mental health.* New York: Basic Books.

James, W. (1958). *The varieties of religious experience: A study in human nature.* New York: Penguin.

Koenig, H. G. (1997). *Is religion good for your health? The effects of religion on physical and mental health.* New York: Haworth.

Kwilecki, S. (1988). A scientific approach to religious development: Proposals and a case illustration. *Journal for the Scientific Study of Religion, 27,* 307–325.

Kwilecki, S. (1994). Soul-loss and religious consolation in two lives. In R. K. Fenn & D. Capps (Eds.), *On losing the soul: Essays in the social psychology of religion.* Albany: State University of New York Press.

Kwilecki, S. (1999). *Becoming religious: Understanding devotion to the unseen.* Lewisburg, PA: Bucknell University Press.

Matthews, D. A., with Clark, C. (1998). *The faith factor: Proof of the healing power of prayer.* New York: Penguin.

THE INTERNATIONAL JOURNAL FOR THE PSYCHOLOGY OF RELIGION, *10*(1), 47–56

COMMENTARY

Spiritual Intelligence or Spiritual Consciousness?

John D. Mayer

Department of Psychology
University of New Hampshire

Emmons's (this issue) thought-provoking article defined a spiritual intelligence that involves five characteristics:

1. The capacity for transcendence.
2. The ability to enter into heightened spiritual states of consciousness.
3. The ability to invest everyday activities, events, and relationships with a sense of the sacred.
4. The ability to utilize spiritual resources to solve problems in living.
5. The capacity to engage in virtuous behavior or to be virtuous (to show forgiveness, to express gratitude, to be humble, to display compassion).

When I think of spirituality, I think less of a heightened intelligence, as Emmons has described it, and more of a heightened consciousness. The idea of spiritual consciousness stems from the possibility of structuring consciousness, through meditation, contemplation, and other means, so that it focuses on oneness, transcendent states, and ultimate concerns. The shift in language from the terminology of mental ability (mentioned earlier) to one of consciousness and awareness yields an interesting revision of Emmons's description. This spiritual consciousness would involve

---

Requests for reprints should be sent to John D. Mayer, Department of Psychology, University of New Hampshire, Durham, NH 03824.

1. *Attending* to the unity of the world and transcending one's existence.
2. *Consciously entering* into heightened spiritual states.
3. *Attending* to the sacred in everyday activities, events, and relationships.
4. *Structuring consciousness* so that problems in living are seen in the context of life's ultimate concerns.
5. *Desiring* to act, and consequently, acting in virtuous ways (to show forgiveness, to express gratitude, to be humble, to display compassion).

To translate from the language of intelligence to the language of consciousness, it would seem, requires substituting just a few key words for the terms *ability* and *capacity*, that were in the original. So, which conception is right: spiritual intelligence or spiritual consciousness?

If a new intelligence really has been found, it would enrich and broaden our notion of what intelligence may be (e.g., Mayer, Salovey, & Caruso, in press). Labeling something an intelligence also raises its prestige. Scarr (1989) has argued that one reason psychologists and educators are motivated to label something an intelligence is in an attempt to adjust social behavior to value the entity more than before. Although Scarr believes many personality attributes are not valued sufficiently, she is concerned that labeling nonintelligences as intelligences creates a leveling of all qualities, and a diminishment of the concept of intelligence. So, what is the difference between finding an intelligence and simply labeling something an intelligence?

WITH WHAT YARDSTICK SHOULD SPIRITUAL INTELLIGENCE BE MEASURED?

To me, the term *intelligence* refers to a capacity or ability that primarily concerns performing valid abstract reasoning with coherent symbol systems. This *abstract reasoning* criterion overlaps only partly with the eight criteria of an intelligence, originally developed by Gardner (1993, pp. 62–68), and used by Emmons to assess spiritual intelligence. The "abstract reasoning" criterion represents a more classical approach to intelligence: Symposia on intelligence over the years repeatedly conclude that the first hallmark of intelligence is the capacity to carry out abstract reasoning (Sternberg, 1997). Such thinking involves the ability to carry out many types of mental transformations, such as identifying similarities and differences, making generalizations, mentally rotating figures, and other tasks, all according to specifiable rules (e.g., Carroll, 1993).

By contrast, only one or two of Gardner's (1993, pp. 62–68) eight criteria, his "core mental operations," and perhaps his "symbol system" requirement, approximate abstract reasoning. The remaining six criteria are a combination of cultural, empirical, and other characteristics. Because the criteria are each equally weighted, abstract reasoning is relatively deemphasized. Gardner acknowledged it is unclear how many criteria, and which among them, an entity must meet for it to be labeled an intelligence. Gardner (1993) wrote, "At present the selection (or rejection) of a candidate intelligence is reminiscent more of an artistic judgment than of a scientific assessment" (p. 63).

In this commentary, I focus on how well Emmons's spiritual intelligence meets the abstract reasoning criterion for intelligence I have described. Emmons's theory is young enough that his empirical work on the subject requires time to develop. Still, so as to consider its future development, it is worth mentioning it must eventually satisfy empirical criteria as well. For example, new intelligences must be translatable into mental performance, with agreed upon criteria for correct performance. That is, a person possessing the intelligence should be able to solve specifiable problems that someone without it cannot. Such an intelligence must also satisfy a number of correlational criteria. For example, it must encompass a reasonable number of important areas of thought, in the way that verbal intelligence, say, spans vocabulary, reading comprehension, and verbal fluency. A "History of Dinosaurs" intelligence is a nonstarter because it is simply too limited in scope. Other correlational criteria include that the intelligence is similar enough to other intelligences to be recognizable, but different enough to be worth studying. Finally, the intelligence must develop from infancy to adulthood (e.g., Mayer, Caruso, & Salovey, 1999).

To return to the conceptual: Does spiritual intelligence primarily involve abstract reasoning? I begin with an informal concern—that, traditionally, spirituality is viewed as a form of consciousness, and that spiritual intelligence is not highly distinguishable from spirituality itself. Then I will move on to a more formal consideration of Emmons's five areas of spiritual intelligence and their relation to abstract reasoning and other attributes within personality.

SPIRITUALITY, SPIRITUAL INTELLIGENCE, AND COGNITION: SOME PRELIMINARY OBSERVATIONS

Spirituality, as traditionally understood, seems better characterized by consciousness than by abstract reasoning. For example, one research group has defined spirituality as "a way of being and experiencing that comes about through awareness of a transcendent dimension and that is characterized by certain identifiable values in regard to self, others, nature, life, and whatever one considers to be the Ultimate" (Elkins, Hedstrom, Hughes, Leaf, & Saunders, 1988, p. 10).

The opening phrase—"a way of being and experiencing" (Elkins et al., 1988, p. 10)—is focused on consciousness. This description also touches three areas of Emmons's spiritual intelligence: transcendence, sacredness (or the Ultimate), and values. This raises the concern that spiritual intelligence is, perhaps, a relabeling of spirituality. Consider children who feel spiritual with every part of themselves; who talk to imagined or (some would say) real divine presences far more easily than adults. They have taken a leap of imaginative purity that would confound most adults. Whether such children are intelligent, however, seems irrelevant to their conscious experience of spirituality.

To be sure, some cognition (and therefore, intelligence) is present in all mental life. Praying for the health and welfare of one's family requires knowledge of what "health," "family," and "welfare" are. Cognition is not, however, primary in such instances, and we would expect the person praying to attend to spiritual matters but not necessarily to possess high intelligence in order to pray. My point is that intelligence does not exist simply because some cognition is present, but rather, abstract reasoning must be primary. Consider the realm of artificial intelligence. We usually attribute intelligence to those machines that reach a critical mass of cognitive processing, such as a general-purpose computer that can solve a variety of problems or a computer dedicated to a mentally demanding activity such as playing chess. By comparison, a television is not primarily distinguished by its intelligence, even though it certainly processes information and might even contain a "smart chip" that permits it to solve certain limited problems.

A MORE FORMAL ANALYSIS OF SPIRITUAL INTELLIGENCE

Perhaps such preliminary objections to spiritual intelligence are insufficiently considered. To find out if that is the case requires a more formal discussion of how basic mental mechanisms are characterized. In the next section, I discuss three types of personality components: (a) a diverse variety of low-level mental mechanisms that include motivations, emotions, cognition, and consciousness; (b) learned models of the world; (c) and traits. I compare Emmons's five parts of spiritual intelligence (e.g., transcendence, coping, etc.) to various personality parts to see the degree each one qualifies as engaging valid abstract reasoning.

WHERE IS SPIRITUALITY AMONG THE PARTS OF PERSONALITY?

Elsewhere, I have argued that there exists an extremely heterogeneous class of personality parts that include basic, brain-related mechanisms or modes of processing. These are variously called enablers or enabling mechanisms because they enable human personality to operate (e.g., Averill, 1992; Mayer, 1995; Mayer, Chabot, & Carlsmith, 1997). Each class reflects distinct mental operations, as measured by psychometric and experimental methods; moreover, each class roughly corresponds to the excitation of distinct brain regions (see Hilgard, 1980; MacLean, 1973; Mayer, Chabot, & Carlsmith, 1997, for reviews).

These enablers can be divided into four broad categories, which include cognition, motives, emotions, and consciousness. At this near-brain level, it is possible to separate out something like a pure motive (e.g., thirst), a pure feeling (e.g., sadness), a pure mental capacity (e.g., the capacity to remember digits), and pure consciousness (e.g., awareness of being alive). Each one of these areas of function can itself be broken down into a still-heterogeneous area of activity. For example, motives such as hunger and thirst pertain to metabolic function whereas motives such as the need for affiliation or aggression pertain to social function. Similarly, cognition involves both verbal and spatial reasoning, which may involve different areas of the brain (e.g., Kosslyn et al., 1999). As a first approximation, however, it makes sense to talk about the broad, biologically related classes of motives, emotions, cognitions, and consciousness.

Motives, emotions, or cognitions rarely operate on their own, however, but rather blend together to some degree. They join in two ways: first, at the near-biological level itself and then as they are synthesized when a person learns and thinks about the world. At the near-biological level, the four classes of enablers are interconnected and act on one another. Table 1 shows some ways that a given motive, emotion, cognition, or conscious activity (listed down the left-hand side) acts upon another (as listed across the top). For example, we can think of consciousness acting on emotion—to make it felt, attended to, examined. Similarly, we can think of an emotion, such as fear, acting on consciousness to narrow it down to self-preservation.

Enablers stay relatively unchanged in terms of function and purpose throughout the life span. At the same time, by virtue of operating in a changing, growing mind, they can become enhanced, or guided, in some ways. Thus, short-term memory can be enhanced by learning mnemonics (i.e., memory tricks). Consciousness appears able to guide or steer itself through the use of self-suggestion, the influence of current concerns, meditative practices, and other procedures (e.g., Csikszentmihalyi, 1990; Ornstein, 1972). Such directed consciousness seems to describe Emmons's first aspect of spiritual intelligence, transcendence. Transcendence includes such qualities as leaving behind physicality, and sensing bonds with humanity. This seems, to me, close to what psychologists call "structuring," or "developing" consciousness, as opposed to cognition; such structuring guides a person's attention to certain mental phenomena (e.g., breathing, oneness) until the conscious state is altered. Similarly, Emmons's second manifestation of spiritual intelligence, mysticism, seems explicable this way. Mysticism involves entering spiritual states of consciousness in which, through the use of special rituals and prayer, one may become especially contemplative, have flashes of insight, or even see visions. Thus, both transcendence and mysticism appear primarily to involve highly structured con-

TABLE 1
Potential Actions On One Another of Motives, Emotions, Cognitions, and Consciousness

System That Acts	System That is Acted Upon			
	Motivation	*Emotion*	*Cognition*	*Consciousness*
Consciousness	Awareness of motivation.	Awareness of emotion; structured openness or closedness to emotion.	Awareness of cognition.	**Consciousness of consciousness: th structuring of awareness.**
Cognition	Motivational intelligence.	Cognitive identification of and understanding of emotion (emotional intelligence-a).	**Cognitive intelligence.**	Cognitive understanding of consciousness.
Emotion	Emotional amplification of motivation (e.g., happiness and altruism).	**Emotional feeling basic feelings: happy, sad, angry, etc.**	Emotional facilitation of cognition (emotional intelligence-b) and emotional biasing of cognition (e.g., confusion).	Emotional narrowing and expanding, and/oi filtering of consciousness.
Motivation	**Motivational direction (e.g., hunger, thirst).**	Motivation-triggered emotions (e.g., aggression and anger); motivational need for emotion (e.g., need for emotion).	Motivations of cogition (e.g., need for cognition).	Motivational cuing of consciousness.

scious processes, with cognition providing a supporting role by representing the things that must be transcended or contemplated, but with little requirement for abstract reasoning.

As people learn about themselves and the world, they create mental models of reality that integrate motives, emotions, cognitions, and consciousness in another way. These models form a second broad class of personality components different from the enablers in that they are primarily mental representations rather than operations; they are maps or concepts of the self or the world. For example, a man may develop a mental model of Kalamazoo, Michigan, that includes a need to visit the city (a motive), a love of Kalamazoo's Western Michigan University, his alma mater (an emotion), an understanding of the grid of streets and best places to go (cognition), and attention to articles and news about Kalamazoo that most people do not share (consciousness). These models are learned representations, called by such diverse names as establishments (Mayer, 1995, 1998; Murray & Kluckhorn, 1956); schemas (Markus, 1997); personal constructs (Kelly, 1955); scripts, plans, and goals (Schank & Abelson, 1977); and others.

There certainly is abstract reasoning involved in mental representations of spiritual learning. A person's expert knowledge of religious texts and spiritual practices are involved in any spiritual exercise or experience. Scholarship in religious texts such as the Hebrew Bible and New Testament, the Qu'ran, the Bhagavad Gita, and other similar works may heighten a sense of sacredness and transcendence. The third and fourth aspects of Emmons's spiritual intelligence are sanctification and coping. Sanctification involves joining everyday activities with a sense of the sacred. Spiritual coping involves using sacred meanings to find purposes in setbacks and challenges, and to assist one in moving forward in life. I suspect these two areas of spiritual intelligence come closest to meeting criteria for abstract reasoning. Although attending to the sacred involves structuring consciousness, it is assisted by an understanding and appreciation for religious stories, mythologies, anecdotes, and interpretations. A deep familiarity with such works can connect an everyday family event, such as a meal, with an important story in a spiritual or religious tradition. Similarly, coping in response to a physical illness or frailty may be assisted by consideration of one or another stories from those same spiritual and religious traditions.

Perhaps people higher in the proposed spiritual intelligence would see different, more abstract relationships to the sacred than those lower in intelligence. Whether such abstract connections are unique to spiritual literature or would extend to areas of literary scholarship, knowledge of the visual arts, and others, however, is an empirical question. If the reasoning in spiritual stories is the same as that employed in literary scholarship or the arts, then all that might be present would be verbal intelligence; if spiritual reasoning were distinct from those other areas, however, it would provide a basis for a spiritual intelligence.

Thus far, we have discussed low-level mechanisms (enablers) and learned models (establishments). As these interact, mental life exhibits various patterns or themes. For example, a woman's emotional mechanisms (enablers) might generate love, and this love might enter into mental models of her husband, her children, her neighbors, her city, and her possessions, as well as other loves. These emergent patterns or themes can be viewed as a third broad class of personality parts, variously called traits or themes. In the aforementioned example, we may characterize the woman as loving, or warm.

The fifth aspect of spiritual intelligence involves virtuous traits. These include behaving so as to convey forgiveness, gratitude, humility, and mercy. I greatly admire such qualities, yet there are large noncognitive components to them. For example, it is possible to forgive indiscriminately and to express gratitude inappropriately, or unyieldingly. This happens, for instance, when a person repeatedly expresses gratitude for things done, not on his or her behalf, but out of general necessity, or even without him or her in mind.

I worry that to equate forgiveness or gratitude with intelligence is to blur some important distinctions between intellectual and nonintellectual qualities. For example, I would have some reservations about labeling people with happy, easy-going temperaments as spiritually intelligent, because they inherited a temperament that makes it easy for them to forgive others. Similarly, some lucky individuals may forgive others because they have experienced such good treatment throughout life that a few transgressions are easily overlooked. On the other hand, there are people who may find it quite difficult to forgive others, independent of a spiritual intelligence (as I might conceive of it). I am thinking of people whose biological temperament predisposes them to be unhappy and angry, as well as people who have been victimized by such crimes as child abuse and rape, or who have experienced war or concentration camps. These latter individuals often report that it is next to impossible to forgive those responsible, and yet many of them turn to spirituality in order to live and thrive after such tragedy. To me, intelligence is plastic; it allows a person to consider deeply many lines of thought, and many possible paths of life. Only some of these would include forgiveness or gratitude. Attaching such characteristics together seems to limit the utility and power of intelligence.

IN SEARCH OF A SPIRITUAL INTELLIGENCE

Emmons's spiritual intelligence and its five aspects seem to cover a variety of parts of mental life: from structured aspects of consciousness to nonintellective personality traits. To me, Emmons's proposed spiritual intelligence does not yet meet the criterion of primarily involving abstract reasoning. This does not preclude some future version of the concept from meeting such a conceptual criterion. Then, one could determine whether the intelligence also satisfies necessary empirical criteria. There is no doubt that some spiritual individuals reason, and often with great sophistication. There exist important philosophies of guilt, loving kindness, mercy, humility, and other feelings and their relation to ultimate issues (e.g., Otto, 1950; Peli, 1984). We would need to know more, however, about the unique features of such reasoning before spiritual intelligence can be better understood.

To illustrate what I mean about understanding the reasoning involved in spirituality, consider the recent case of emotional intelligence (e.g., Mayer & Salovey, 1997; Salovey & Mayer, 1990) as a candidate intelligence. Emotions had been studied for centuries before the concept of an emotional intelligence could be fully developed. The idea of emotional intelligence developed from a centuries-old, philosophical literature on the meaning of emotions (e.g., Calhoun & Solomon, 1984; Frank, 1988). It developed, as well, from several decades of more concerted scientific work on the nature of emotion, its language, and its meanings (e.g., Bower, 1981; Buck, 1984; Ortony, Clore, & Collins, 1988; see Clark & Fiske, 1982; Forgas, in press, for reviews). This work culminated, perhaps, with empirical work in artificial intelligence and computer understanding of emotions (Dyer, 1983; Picard, 1997).

Some flavor of the rules discovered in such work can be obtained from considering the fictional character, Jane, who was angry one afternoon at 2 p.m., and ashamed at 3 p.m. Given such information, one could surmise that, in-between her anger and her shame, she may have expressed anger and then thought the better of it, or discovered new information which rendered the anger unjustified and petty-seeming, or simply felt ashamed she was angry—as she often does. One can see it is less likely that in-between she had a wonderful interview with the Queen of England (Mayer, Caruso, & Salovey, 1999). Reasoning like this, I would argue, concerns how one emotion can change into certain emotions but not others, given a specific circumstance. Understanding such rules is as complex and sophisticated, in its own way, as is syllogistic reasoning.

A similar working out of the rules of spiritual intelligence would provide a firmer basis for such a proposed entity. It seems to me, however, that esoteric practices of spirituality, along with the lengthy training necessary to learn certain spiritual practices, has impeded the study of the reasoning that is a part of spirituality. The rules of spirituality, whatever they may be, remain to be elaborated, codified, and understood. As I review works by more intellectually oriented spiritual writers, I see the possibility of codifying such thought, but, to the best of my knowledge, it has not yet taken place.

A great service could be done in this area by first elucidating the intellectual underpinnings—the abstract reasoning—involved in spirituality. We must understand the symbol system of spiritual and religious writing better to understand the sort of reasoning that takes place within it. What are the mental transformations necessary to think spiritually? Can the rules of such reasoning be made accessible to the scientist, to computer representations? Are there special instances when spiritual thought achieves a critical mass of abstract reasoning, and therefore qualifies as an intelligence? At present, spiritual intelligence, like spirituality itself, remains mysterious in many respects. As Emmons pursues his journey of describing a spiritual intelligence, I look forward to what he will teach us about the quality of thought that accompanies spirituality.

REFERENCES

Averill, J. R. (1992). The structural bases of emotional behavior: A metatheoretical analysis. *Review of Personality and Social Psychology, 13,* 1-24.

Bower, A. T. (1981). Mood and memory. *American Psychologist, 36,* 129-148.

Buck, R. (1984). *The communication of emotion.* New York: Guilford.

Calhoun, C., & Solomon, R. C. (Eds.). (1984). *What is an emotion?: Classic readings in philosophical psychology.* New York: Oxford University Press.

Carroll, J. B. (1993). *Human cognitive abilities: A survey of factor-analytic studies.* New York: Cambridge University Press.

Clark, M. S., & Fiske, S. T. (1982). *Affect and cognition: The 17th Annual Carnegie Symposium on Cognition.* Hillsdale, NJ: Lawrence Erlbaum Associates, Inc.

Csikszentmihalyi, M. (1990). *Flow: The psychology of optimal experience*. New York: HarperCollins.

Dyer, M.G. (1983). The role of affect in narratives. *Cognitive Science, 7,* 211–242.

Elkins, D. N., Hedstrom, L. J., Hughes, L. L., Leaf, J. A., & Saunders, C. L. (1988). Toward a humanistic–phenomenological spirituality: Definition, description, and measurement. *Journal of Humanistic Psychology, 28,* 5–18.

Forgas, J. P. (in press). *Handbook of affect and social cognition.* Mahwah, NJ: Lawrence Erlbaum Associates, Inc.

Frank, R. H. (1988). *Passions with reason: The strategic role of the emotions.* New York: Norton.

Gardner, H. (1993). *Frames of mind: The theory of multiple intelligences.* New York: Basic Books.

Hilgard, E. R. (1980). The trilogy of mind: Cognition, affection, and conation. *Journal of the History of the Behavioral Sciences, 16,* 107–117.

Kelly, G.A. (1955). *The psychology of personal constructs* (Vol. 1). New York: Norton.

Kosslyn, S. M., Pascual-Leone, A., Felician, O., Camposano, S., Keenan, J. P., Thompson, W. L., Ganis, G., Sukel, K. E., & Alpert, N. M. (1999). The role of Area 17 in visual imagery: Convergent evidence from PET and rTMS. *Science, 284,* 167–170.

MacLean, P. D. (1973). *A triune concept of the brain and behavior.* Toronto: University of Toronto Press.

Markus, H. (1977). Self-schemata and processing information about the self. *Journal of Personality and Social Psychology, 35,* 63–78.

Mayer, J. D. (1995). A framework for the classification of personality components. *Journal of Personality, 63,* 819–877.

Mayer, J. D. (1998). A systems framework for the field of personality psychology. *Psychological Inquiry, 9,* 118–144.

Mayer, J. D. (in press). Emotion, intelligence, emotional intelligence: Individual differences in hot processing. In J. P. Forgas (Ed.), *The handbook of affect and social cognition.* Mahwah, NJ: Lawrence Erlbaum Associates, Inc.

Mayer, J. D., Caruso, D., & Salovey, P. (1999). Emotional intelligence meets traditional standards for an intelligence. *Intelligence.*

Mayer, J. D., Chabot, H. F., & Carlsmith, K. (1997). Conation, affect, and cognition in personality. In G. Matthews (Ed.), *Cognitive science perspectives on personality and emotion* (pp. 31–63). Amsterdam: Elsevier.

Mayer, J. D., & Salovey, P. (1997). What is emotional intelligence? In P. Salovey & D. Sluyter (Eds.), *Emotional development and emotional intelligence: Implications for educators* (pp. 3–31). New York: Basic Books.

Mayer, J. D., Salovey, P., & Caruso, D. R. (in press). Competing models of emotional intelligence. In R. J. Sternberg (Ed.), *Handbook of human intelligence* (2nd ed.; pp. 3–44).

Murray, H. A., & Kluckhorn, C. (1956). Outline of a conception of personality. In C. Kluckhorn & H. A. Murray (Eds.), *Personality in nature, society, and culture* (2nd ed.). New York: Knopf.

Ornstein, R. (1972). *The psychology of consciousness.* New York: Viking Penguin.

Ortony, A., Clore, G. L., & Collins, A. (1988). *Cognitive structure of emotions.* New York: Cambridge University Press.

Otto, R. (1950). *The idea of the holy* (2nd ed.). New York: Oxford University Press.

Peli, P. (1984). *Soloveitchik on repentance.* New York: Paulist Press.

Picard, R. W. (1997). *Affective computing.* Cambridge, MA: MIT Press.

Salovey, P., & Mayer, J. D. (1990). Emotional intelligence. *Imagination, Cognition, and Personality, 9,* 185–211.

Scarr, S. (1989). Protecting general intelligence: Constructs and consequences for intervention. In R. L. Linn (Ed.), *Intelligence: Measurement, theory, and public policy.* Urbana: University of Illinois Press.

Schank, R. C., & Abelson, R. P. (1977). *Scripts, plans, goals, and understanding.* Hillsdale, NJ: Lawrence Erlbaum Associates, Inc.

Sternberg, R. J. (1997). The concept of intelligence and its role in lifelong learning and success. *American Psychologist, 52,* 1030–1045.

THE INTERNATIONAL JOURNAL FOR THE PSYCHOLOGY OF RELIGION, *10*(1), 57–64

RESPONSE

Spirituality and Intelligence: Problems and Prospects

Robert A. Emmons

Department of Psychology
University of California, Davis

According to my reading, the three commentators to my article have answered the question I posed "Is Spirituality an Intelligence?" in the following ways: A qualified "no" (Gardner, this issue), a qualified "yes" (Kwilecki, this issue), and "perhaps" (Mayer, this issue). My goal in writing the article was to provoke discussion and debate about the legitimacy of the concept of spiritual intelligence, and to engage in a dialogue over the composition of spiritual intelligence and its implications for psychology and religion. It was with a fair amount of trepidation that I read the commentaries, for this was my initial foray into the uncharted waters of spiritual intelligence. My worst fear was that the idea would appear either blatantly obvious or ridiculously absurd. I am comforted that neither extreme appears to have been the case. The enterprise was described as "thought-provoking" (Mayer) as "eminently reasonable and plausible ... meriting further examination" (Gardner) and "has much to recommend" (Kwilecki).

I am overwhelmingly grateful for the thought that the three commentators put into their responses, and I found their replies encouraging, enlightening, and challenging. Their insights and criticisms have suggested areas where I might clarify points made in the target article. Beyond clarification, however, they raise important issues for the larger endeavor of attempting to link spirituality and religiousness with intelligence and life functioning. Clearly, there are many unresolved

Requests for reprints should be sent to Robert A. Emmons, Department of Psychology, University of California, One Shields Avenue, Davis, CA 95616–8686. E-mail: raemmons@ucdavis.edu questions regarding attempts to tether spirituality and intelligence, and the field of the psychology of religion can only profit from the astute insights raised by this distinguished trio of commentators.

Given their diversity in background and field of expertise (education and cognitive psychology, personality psychology, and religious studies) it is not surprising that each commentator raised unique concerns about the spiritual intelligence framework. Rather than attempt to extract common themes and discuss them sequentially, I will respond separately to each commentator's piece, pointing out convergences across the essays where possible. Space limitations prevent me from responding to all of the points raised. Instead, I will focus on those that I see as most central to the future status of spirituality as an intelligence.

MAYER: SPIRITUAL INTELLIGENCE OR SPIRITUAL CONSCIOUSNESS?

Mayer (this issue), along with his colleague, Salovey, has for several years been developing the concept of emotional intelligence (EI). *EI* is the ability to perceive and express emotion, to assimilate emotion in thought, to understand and reason with emotion, and to regulate emotion in self and others (Mayer, Caruso, & Salovey, 1999). Psychologists who study emotion should be indebted to Mayer and Salovey for demonstrating that emotion and reason are not only not incompatible with each other, but also that emotion may facilitate cognitive functioning. Their work on EI fortified my own thinking about the intellectual underpinnings of spiritual intelligence. The concept of EI has become popularized and marketed by the establishment over the past few years so that it barely resembles the original formulation. However, to the credit of Mayer and his colleagues, they have continued to do the painstaking work of determining whether EI actually meets the accepted criteria for an intelligence, and developing innovative, performance-based measures of EI.

I have appreciated Mayer's careful analysis of the construct of intelligence in developing a research program for determining whether EI meets traditional standards for an intelligence. According to Mayer, three stringent criteria must be met in order for a candidate intelligence to be judged a true intelligence. First, intelligence must reflect mental performance rather than just preferred ways of behaving. We do not yet have measures of spiritual-related abilities, but I am in strong agreement with Mayer that such measures be performance-based. Second, the intelligence should define a set of abilities that are moderately intercorrelated with one another. Third, the intelligence develops with age and experience, from childhood to adulthood. In support of the second and third criteria, it has been argued that spiritual capacities are highly interdependent and that the development of one fosters the development of others (Walsh & Vaughan, 1993), and that spiritual capacities are age-related (Weibust & Thomas, 1994).

In his commentary, Mayer raised the question of whether the construct I describe should best be characterized as "spiritual consciousness" rather than a "spiritual intelligence." In so doing, Mayer tapped into a deep tradition within transpersonal psychology that speaks of concepts such as "spiritual enlightenment," "spiritual illumination," "cosmic consciousness," and "unity consciousness" (see Weibust & Thomas, 1994, for a review). Mayer is concerned with the possible conflation of spirituality (or spiritual consciousness) with spiritual intelligence, and for good reason. If spiritual intelligence were nothing more than spirituality, then nothing would be gained by invoking the language of intelligence. Is spiritual intelligence nothing more than spirituality? I have defined spiritual intelligence as the adaptive use of spiritual information to facilitate everyday problem solving and goal attainment. Spirituality is a broader, more encompassing construct that has as its focus a search for the sacred. It is a search for experience that is meaningful in and of itself. Intelligence is the implementation of a set of tools to arrive at a more productive, effective, happier, and ultimately more meaningful life; spirituality determines how "meaningful" is defined. Spiritual intelligence is thus a mechanism by which people can improve their overall quality of life. It is the application of a domain of knowledge to problems in living. Spiritual intelligence, as promotive of well-being, is largely a positive, adaptive construct whereas spirituality may be positive or negative depending on how it is expressed in particular contexts. As Gardner suggested in his description of charismatic religious leaders, those same skills might be applied inappropriately in a destructive manner.

Mayer also questioned whether the abilities that I have conceptualized as virtues—to show forgiveness, express gratitude, be humble, display compassion—really belong in a domain of personality that is fundamentally different from cognitive competencies and abilities. I admit that this is the component of spiritual intelligence about which I have the most reservations. Virtues, however, can be practiced; they are skill-like dispositions or capacities that can be cultivated and strengthened. Thus, they are more than merely preferences. They are spiritual in that they are viewed as highly prized possessions in all of the major religions of the world, and have qualified (in my mind) as elements of spiritual intelligence as they are involved in intelligent living and contribute to life competence (e.g., to give up a grudge is generally viewed as the smart thing to do, to acknowledge gratitude for the gifts one has received is similarly wise). Admittedly, retaining them in a model of spiritual intelligence results in what Mayer, Caruso, and Salovey (1999) have characterized as a "mixed-model" of intelligence, where mental abilities, dispositions, and traits are included in a compound collection of ingredients. Future empirical work will need to determine whether these traitlike qualities belong in the model, or even whether they covary among themselves. Conceptually cogent arguments have been made for the unity of the virtues (Roberts, 1995), and it is an active area of discussion in the subfield of virtue ethics within moral philosophy. Gardner also found the inclusion of these proclivities problematic, for he believes that they lead to a conflation between a descriptive and a prescriptive social science.

In light of these cogent arguments, I am willing to (at least for now) take the conservative route and remove the "capacity to engage in virtuous behavior" from the list of the core components of spiritual intelligence. Although I maintain that these characteristics often lead to intelligent living and effectiveness, they are not part and parcel of a mental abilities conception of intelligence. Certainly there are those individuals who have the capacity for forgiveness and other virtues who do not necessarily have developed other spiritual competencies, nor have a particular interest in religion or spirituality as a domain of expertise. Eliminating this component enables a stronger argument to be made for spiritual intelligence as a set of abilities rather than preferred courses of behavior (Mayer et al., 1999).

KWILECKI: SPIRITUAL INTELLIGENCE AS A THEORY OF INDIVIDUAL RELIGION

I am greatly indebted to Kwilecki (this issue) for her application of the spiritual intelligence framework to the life of a single individual, Gladys Day. The study of individual lives has enjoyed a long and distinguished tradition in my field, personality psychology, and the concrete illustration provided by Kwilecki is a welcome relief from the theoretical abstractions in my article. Not surprisingly, I am encouraged to see that the core components of spiritual intelligence were identifiable in the life of Gladys Day. She is also a powerful example of Gardner's multiple intelligences theory, providing proof that low levels of intelligence as conventionally conceived are not reflective of high levels of functioning in other areas of the intellect. I also appreciate Kwilecki's (this issue) clear conception of spirituality as "devotion to transcendent forces credited with ultimacy" (p. 35) and personal spirituality as "an expression of a generic human potential for transcendence" (p. 42). As psychologists continue to debate the meanings of spirituality and religiousness, Kwilecki reminds us that there is much to be gained from a dialogue with our colleagues in theology and religious studies. I am reminded, also, that intelligence is a key theological concept in certain (e.g., Latter Day Saint) theologies.

I would not necessarily expect the construct of spiritual intelligence to account for the lion's share of the variance in Gladys Day's behavior, however, because prediction and explanation requires constructs at multiple levels of analysis. For example, although her spiritual sensitivities, ultimate concerns, and virtuous character traits might produce behavioral regularities across situations and over time in her life, these are not independent of temperament, socialization history, cultural context, psychopathological states, and other influencing factors.

Kwilecki made an important point that speaks to the current ground swell of interest in predicting life outcomes from measures of religiousness and spirituality.

She wrote "he joins with a growing number of contemporary researchers impressed by the prophylactic and remedial power of religion across all manner of human ills." She regards this as an "oversimplification, a misguided effort to sanitize religion, an oversimplification of an inherently paradoxical reality." I made the point in my article that even though I was highlighting religion's role in adjustment, "I am not denying that there is a nonfunctional quality to faith that is not explicable in purely utilitarian terms." Certainly religion needs no applied apologetic. In defense of those authors she cites, it should be pointed out that the majority do acknowledge ways in which religious and spiritual lifestyles harm as well as heal (e.g., Koenig, 1997, chap. 7). It is interesting to note, however, that the recent resurgence of interest in the psychology of religion is due in no small part to empirical demonstrations that religious and spiritual variables *matter* for conventional physical and mental health outcomes and end points (Ellison & Levin, 1998). It is the demonstration of these robust associations that has increased the credibility and respectability of research on religion and spirituality within the social and health sciences.

The primary value of Kwilecki's analysis, in my mind, lies in her distinction between secular and spiritual concepts of the good life. I am certainly sympathetic with this argument. In my book, *The Psychology of Ultimate Concerns: Motivation and Spirituality in Personality* (Emmons, 1999), I not only argued for the distinctiveness of spiritual strivings, but also that conventional indices of psychological well-being such has happiness and life satisfaction may be insufficient as outcomes to measure the impact of spiritual striving. Spirituality may promote healthy functioning in some realms of life while straining functioning in others. I suggest that intrapersonal integration, measured in terms of systemic harmony between one's goals, might particularly be one outcome that is highly valued in both secular and religious traditions. Very little research has been conducted on personality integration and well-being, yet I believe that it is a promising line of inquiry. At its core, religion offers nothing less than the transformation of the person from fragmentation to integration, from separation to reconciliation. Streng (1976) defined religion as a "means of ultimate transformation" (p. 7), and noted that "religious awareness brings people to the most comprehensive awareness possible in any given moment" (p. 8). Such awareness, rather than being comforting, can also be experienced as unpleasant, and Kwilecki urged us not to overlook this paradoxical aspect of spiritual knowing.

I would contend that although clearly differing in method, bringing about unity in the person, rescuing the psyche from inner turmoil and conflict, is the purpose of both theologically and psychologically based interventions. Religion invests human existence with meaning by establishing goals and value systems that pertain to all aspects of a person's life with the potential to confer unity on discordant impulses and strivings. The emerging discipline of "positive psychology" (Seligman, 1998) has begun to systematically explore what constitutes "the good life," and one inevitable outcome of this work will be a reexamination of traditional ways of thinking about adaptiveness, life success, and optimal living. As Kwilecki reminds us, a neglect of a spiritual or religious framework in these endeavors is likely to be a serious omission.

GARDNER: A CASE AGAINST SPIRITUAL INTELLIGENCE

Given that it was Gardner's theory of multiple intelligences that provoked my interest in exploring spirituality as a type of intelligence, I was particularly interested in his reaction to the target article. He did not disappoint. Gardner (this issue) touched on many different themes in his article, some of which overlap with concerns raised by Mayer and Kwilecki. Gardner attributed some of the differences between his position and mine to our different intellectual styles: He fancied himself as "an inveterate splitter," while diagnosing me as "an avid lumper" (p. 32). Guilty as charged. Most personality psychologists worth their salt tend to be lumpers. After all, it is the field of personality that, perhaps more than any area of psychology, exploits the "lumping" of statistical techniques of factor analysis and cluster analysis. I prefer to depict our differences using different terminology, however. In the language of cognitive neuroscience, Howard Gardner, I suspect, tends to more frequently employ the "reductionistic operator" (d'Aquili & Newberg, 1999) whereas I may be more likely to employ the "holistic operator." Cognitive operators, according to d'Aquili and Newberg, comprise the most basic functions of the mind. They represent neural networks that operate upon sensate experience to organize and elaborate it in ways that may enable us to respond to internal and external demands. The holistic operator allows the perception of the global or unitary perspective whereas the reductionistic operator analyzes the component parts and is thus associated with analytical processing. Moreover, understanding reality involves a dialectic between the holistic and reductionistic approaches, leaving room for both "lumping" and "splitting."

A very important distinction is made between an intelligence and a domain. An intelligence, according to Gardner, is "a biological potential to analyze certain kinds of information in certain ways." A domain, on the other hand, is "an organized activity in a culture wherein one can rank individuals in terms of their relative expertise." This distinction helps clarify the difference between spirituality and spiritual intelligence. Religion, or spirituality, is thus a domain marked by concern with sacred, transcendent realities. Spiritual intelligence is a biological potential to utilize the domain of spiritual information to facilitate problem solving. It is resource that can be brought to bear upon problems in living. Gardner raised several intriguing questions about how these spiritual resources are drawn upon and may lead to better problem solving. Although I cannot offer definitive answers to these questions, I suspect that the work of Pargament and his colleagues on religious problem solving (Pargament, 1997) may offer important clues concerning spiritual resources in problem solving. Pargament has empirically identified styles of religious problem solving (deferring, controlling, collaborative) as well as cognitive mechanisms (reframing, sacralization) that enable adaptation in crisis situations. Much more work needs to be done to ascertain how a religious or spiritual way of knowing evokes higher sensitivities to life problems.

Gardner would be more sanguine about the possibility of spiritual intelligence if there existed more "convincing evidence about brain structures and processes dedicated to this form of computation." Brain mapping studies are beginning to identify neural circuitry that generates spiritual states, and a recently published volume by two highly regarded neuroscientists (d'Aquili & Newberg, 1999) reviews the current state of knowledge on the neurobiological basis of mystical and religious experience. The evidence is pointing in the direction of neural systems that enable religious ways of knowing. Yet Gardner asked the legitimate question of whether this neural circuitry has evolved for religious experience or for some other purpose that has yet to be determined. The alteration of religious–mystical experience in certain brain disorders (Saver & Rabin, 1997) provides additional evidence for the existence of spiritual mental capacities, and Gardner (1993) stated that "the consequences of brain injury may well constitute the single most instructive line of evidence regarding those distinctive abilities or computations that lie at the core of a human intelligence" (p. 63). In a recent study of persons with Alzheimer disease, McFadden, Ingram, and Baldauf (in press) observed many exemplars of spiritual intelligence in the lives of these people despite severe neurological damage.

CONCLUSION

Let me reiterate my purpose in writing the target article. I wished to initiate a serious dialogue on possible overlap between the constructs of intelligence and spirituality, terms that are not often uttered in the same breath. Given the high level of the commentaries, the target article appears to have been successful. Serious dialogue can only profit the scientific study of spirituality. I defend my original premise that there exist a set of skills and abilities associated with spirituality that are relevant to everyday problem solving (whether we call them spiritual intelligence or spiritual consciousness), and that individual differences in these skills constitute core features of the person. Furthermore, the study of intelligence can produce fresh insights into understanding the overall functioning of spirituality in people's lives as they negotiate their life tasks. I am not suggesting that spirituality can be reduced to intelligence, or even to a set of cognitive abilities and capacities. I maintain that spirituality meets the criteria for an intelligence as outlined in Gardner's theory of multiple intelligences. In light of the commentaries, I have proposed a modification to the original list of core components of spiritual intelligence to now consist of four: (a) the capacity for transcendence, (b) the ability to enter into heightened spiritual states of consciousness, (c) the ability to invest everyday activities, events, and relationships with a sense of the sacred or divine, and (d) the ability to utilize spiritual resources to solve problems in living. The question "is spirituality an intelligence?" may not even be answerable as it is posed. We need to ask more specific questions about the nature of the mental abilities involved. But it is a concept relevant to a "lived" spirituality, as the life of Gladys Day illustrates. Given the multifaceted nature of spirituality, we need all of the theoretical tools at our disposal because any one approach is inherently limited.

REFERENCES

d'Aquili, E., & Newberg, A. B. (1999). *The mystical mind: Probing the biology of religious experience.* Minneapolis, MN: Fortress Press.

Ellison, C. G., & Levin, J. S. (1998). The religion–health connection: Evidence, theory, and future directions. *Health Education and Behavior, 25,* 700–720.

Emmons, R. A. (1999). *The psychology of ultimate concerns: Motivation and spirituality in personality.* New York: Guilford.

Gardner, H. (1993). *Frames of mind: The theory of multiple intelligences.* New York: Basic Books.

Koenig, H. G. (1997). *Is religion good for your health? The effects of religion on physical and mental health.* New York: Haworth.

Mayer, J. D., Caruso, D. R., & Salovey, P. (1999). Emotional intelligence meets traditional standards for an intelligence. *Intelligence.*

McFadden, S. H., Ingram, M., & Baldauf, C. (in press). Actions, feelings, and values: Foundations of meaning and personhood in dementia. *Journal of Religious Gerontology.*

Pargament, K. I. (1997). *The psychology of religion and coping.* New York: Guilford.

Roberts, R. C. (1995). Forgivingness. *American Philosophical Quarterly, 32,* 289–306.

Saver, J. L., & Rabin, J. (1997). The neural substrates of religious experience. *The Journal of Neuropsychiatry and Clinical Neurosciences, 9,* 498–510.

Seligman, M. E. (1998, April). Positive social science. *APA Monitor, 29,* 2, 5.

Streng, F. J. (1976). *Understanding religious life* (2nd ed.). Encino, CA: Dickenson.

Walsh, R., & Vaughan, F. (1993). The art of transcendence: An introduction to common elements of transpersonal practices. *The Journal of Transpersonal Psychology, 25,* 1–9.

Weibust, P. S., & Thomas, L. E. (1994). Learning and spirituality in adulthood. In J. D. Sinnott (Ed.), *Interdisciplinary handbook of adult life span learning* (pp. 120–134). Westport, CT: Greenwood.

www.ingramcontent.com/pod-product-compliance
Ingram Content Group UK Ltd.
Pitfield, Milton Keynes, MK11 3LW, UK
UKHW020427010325